SCIENCE DETECTIVE™
Beginning

Higher-Order
Thinking·Reading·Writing
in Science

SERIES TITLES

Science Detective™ Beginning

Science Detective™ A1

Stephen Fischer and Joseph Carroll

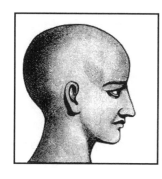

© 2004
THE CRITICAL THINKING CO.
(BRIGHT MINDS™)
www.CriticalThinking.com
P.O. Box 1610 • Seaside • CA 93955-1610
Phone 800-458-4849 • FAX 831-393-3277
ISBN 0-89455-834-X
Printed in the United States of America

The authors would like to thank the editors
below for their savvy and their assistance.

Margaret Hockett

Cynthia Alai

Many of the images used in this book are from Nova Development Corporation's Art Explosion Software™, 23801 Calabasas Road, Suite 2005, Calabasas, CA 91302-1547, USA.

Selected images used herein were obtained from IMSI's MasterClips® Premium Image Collection, 1895 Francisco Blvd. East, San Rafael, CA 94901-5506, USA.

TABLE OF CONTENTS

III. EARTH SCIENCE

Introduction

The lessons in this book are designed to improve student skills in science, critical thinking, reading, and writing. The topics and skills covered are drawn from the National Science Education Standards, grades 3-4.

Activity questions require critical thinking and careful reading of text, charts, graphs, and tables. Students are required to explain their thinking in writing.

Students are frequently asked to support their answers with evidence. The evidence requires in-depth analysis of information in the text, diagram, or both. This analysis develops good reading comprehension and critical thinking skills.

Also included is an answer key and a complete chart of the National Science Education Standards through grade 4 and the numbers of the lessons covering each standard.

When to Use The Science Detective™

Science Detective™ can be used to introduce or thoroughly review topics in your science curriculum. *Science Detective*™ is an ideal solution for comprehensive test prep in advance of state science assessments or any assessments that require students to explain and support their answers.

Grades 3–4 Science Standards

The science topics covered in this book are organized around the National Science Education Standards as listed below (for a detailed list of all concepts covered by lesson, see the Skills Chart). Moreover, concepts and terms were derived from a survey of popular elementary science texts.

Physical Science: Students should develop an understanding of

- The properties of objects and materials
- Position and motion of objects
- Light, heat, electricity, and magnetism

Life Science: Students should develop an understanding of

- The characteristics of organisms
- The life cycles of organisms
- Organisms and their environments

Earth and Space Science: Students should develop an understanding of

- The properties of earth materials
- Objects in the sky
- Changes in the earth and sky

All lessons contain important science vocabulary, and all scientific terms commonly found in 3–4 grade science textbooks are included. Some of these terms are defined in the lesson and some must be identified through context clues.

Reading in Science

Many students have trouble reading in general, and do not understand the importance of reading in science. *Science Detective*™ teaches students to read carefully by requiring them to identify evidence that supports their answers. In fact, students must often identify information from multiple sources (text, diagrams, and other graphics) and synthesize these different pieces of information to arrive at the answer. The analysis needed to solve these problems develops thinking skills and greatly improves reading comprehension.

Written Explanations

Many questions in this book ask students to use complete sentences to explain their thinking. The ability to express their thoughts—supported by evidence—in writing, is not only important in science assessment, it is essential when communicating with other people in school and work. It also promotes better understanding of the concepts being studied.

The questions in *Science Detective*™ are modeled after questions found on science assessments but require more critical thinking. There is a growing trend to evaluate responses to open-ended questions in the context of logical reasoning, and many science students score poorly on these test items. The carefully designed questions in *Science Detective*™ will not only develop thinking, reading, and writing skills, but will also familiarize your students with questions found on contemporary science assessments.

Suggestions

Each lesson is formatted as two adjacent pages so that students can easily refer back and forth between questions and content. A student should have little trouble understanding the question or finding a relevant answer from the lesson content. It will be helpful to students if you to do one or two lessons with them: read the lesson out loud and then discuss the questions and the answers.

If a student has trouble communicating the answer to a question, ask her to explain the answer aloud, then guide her on how to write the explanation. A separate introduction has been provided for the student.

It is suggested that you give a fact-oriented quiz to establish closure on the content of each lesson.

SKILLS CHART
National Science Education Standards[1] through grade 4

Physical Science	Lesson
Properties of Objects & Materials	
Objects have many observable properties including size, weight, shape, color, temperature, and the ability to react with other substances.	1
Those properties can be measured using tools, such as rulers, balances, and thermometers.	2
Objects are made of one or more materials, such as paper, wood, and metal. Objects can be described by the properties of the materials from which they are made, and those properties can be used to separate or sort a group of objects or materials.	3
Materials can exist in different states—solid, liquid, and gas.	4
Some common materials, such as water can be changed from one state to another by heating or cooling.	5
Position & Motion of Objects	
The position of an object can be described by locating it relative to another object or the background.	6
The position and motion of objects can be changed by pushing or pulling. The size of the change is related to the strength of the push or pull.	7
Sound is produced by vibrating objects.	8
The pitch of the sound can be varied by changing the rate of vibration.	9
Light, Heat, Electricity, and Magnetism	
Light travels in a straight line until it strikes an object. Light can be reflected by a mirror, refracted by a lens, or absorbed by the object.	10
Heat can be produced in many ways, such as burning, rubbing, or mixing one substance with another. Heat can move from one object to another by conduction.	11
Electricity in circuits can produce light, heat, sound, and magnetic effects.	12
Electrical circuits require a complete loop through which an electrical current can pass.	13
Magnets attract and repel each other and certain kinds of other materials.	14

[1]Reprinted with permission from *The National Science Education Standards* by the National Academies of Sciences, courtesy of The National Academies Press, Washington, D. C.

SKILLS CHART, Continued
National Science Education Standards through grade 4

Life Science	Lesson
The Characteristics of Organisms	
Organisms have basic needs. For example, animals need air, water, and food; plants require water, air, nutrients, and light.	15
Organisms can survive only in environments in which their needs can be met. The world has many different environments, and distinct environments support the life of different types of organisms.	16
Each plant or animal has different structures that serve different functions in growth, survival, and reproduction.	17, 18, 19, 20
The behavior of individual organisms is influenced by internal cues (such as hunger) and by external cues (such as a change in the environment).	20, 21
Humans and other organisms have senses to help them detect internal and external cues.	22
Life Cycles of Organisms	
Plants and animals have life cycles that include being born, developing into adults, reproducing, and eventually dying. The details of this life cycle are different for different organisms.	23, 24
Plants and animals closely resemble their parents. Many characteristics of an organism are inherited from the parents of the organism, but other characteristics result from an individual's interactions with the environment.	25
Organisms and Their Environments	
All animals depend on plants. Some animals eat plants for food. Other animals eat animals that eat the plants. An organism's patterns of behavior are related to the nature of that organism's environment, including the kinds and numbers of other organisms present, the availability of food and resources, and the physical characteristics of the environment. When the environment changes, some plants and animals survive and reproduce, and others die and move to new locations.	26
All organisms cause changes in the environment where they live. Some of these changes are detrimental to the organism or other organisms, whereas others are beneficial.	27
Humans depend on their natural and constructed environments. Humans change environments in ways that can either be beneficial or detrimental for themselves and other organisms.	28

SKILLS CHART, Continued
National Science Education Standards through grade 4

Earth Science	Lesson
Properties of Earth Materials	
Earth materials are solid rocks and soils, water, and the gases of the atmosphere.	29
The varied materials have different physical and chemical properties, which make them useful in different ways, for example, as building materials, as sources of fuel, or for growing the plants we use as food.	30, 31 32, 33
Soils have properties of color and texture, capacity to retain water, and the ability to support the growth of many kinds of plants, including those in our food supply.	33
Fossils provide evidence about the plants and animals that lived long ago and the nature of the environment at that time.	34
Objects in the Sky	
The sun, moon, stars, clouds, birds, and airplanes all have properties, locations, and movements that can be observed and described.	39
The sun provides the light and heat necessary to maintain the temperature of the earth.	40
Changes in the Earth and Sky	
The surface of the earth changes. Some changes are due to slow processes, such as erosion and weathering, and some changes are due to rapid process, such as landslides, volcanic eruptions, and earthquakes.	35, 36
Weather changes from day to day and over the seasons. Weather can be described by measurable quantities, such as temperature, wind direction and speed, and precipitation.	37, 38
Objects in the sky have patterns of movement. The sun, for example, appears to move across the sky in the same way every day, but its path changes slowly over the seasons. The moon moves across the sky on a daily basis much like the sun. The observable shape of the moon changes from day to day in a cycle that lasts about a month.	41

SCORING & ASSESSMENT CRITERIA

Each complete *Science Detective*™ activity includes a lesson and related questions. Questions may require identification of evidence or explanations of a student's thinking. To get a good picture of a student's overall performance, we suggest using a 3-part score: 1) score answers for correctness, 2) score answers for clarity, and 3) score accuracy of evidence cited. Many teachers find the reproducible scoring rubric below to be useful in assessing student performance on these lessons.

✂ --

Student Name _____

Activity _____

SCIENCE DETECTIVE SCORING RUBRIC

• Content (correct answers show understanding of concept)
• Clarity of student's explanations (complete sentences, clearly written)
• Evidence sentences and paragraphs correctly identified

Content: If the information in your answer showed complete understanding of the information in the story and graphics, you got a 3. If it showed a partial understanding, you got a 2 or a 1. If there was no evidence that you understood the information, you got a 0.

Clarity: If you communicated clearly, even if the ideas themselves were wrong, you got a 3. If your ideas were communicated poorly, you got a 1 or 2. If you were not clear and it was not possible to understand your thoughts as written, you got a 0.

Evidence: If you correctly identified all sentences or paragraphs that prove or give the best evidence for your answer, you got a 3. If you identified some of the correct evidence, you got a 1 or 2. If you did not correctly identify any of the evidence, you got a 0.

Content Score: _____ (Scale 0–3)

Clarity Score: _____ (Scale 0–3)

Evidence Score: _____ (Scale 0–3)

Comments:

_____

_____

_____

To the Student

Why You Should Become a Science Detective

Critical thinking, reading, and writing are as important in science as they are in the rest of your subjects. This workbook was created to improve your thinking, reading, and writing skills while you learn science.

It's All About Evidence

As a critical thinker, you need to look for *evidence* in what you read. Evidence is information that shows why something is true or could be true.

Read the six sentences below and try to answer the following question: Is the filament in a flashlight bulb a good conductor? Find the evidence that tells you the answer.

[1]The term **electric current** is used to describe the number of electrons moving through a wire every second. [2]A material that lets electrons pass through it easily is called a conductor.

[3]When electrons flow through the flashlight bulb, they pass through a thin wire called a filament. [4]The filament blocks, or *resists*, the flow of electrons. [5]As electrons are forced through the filament, they produce friction, and friction produces heat. [6]Forcing electrons through a filament produces so much heat that the wire gets white hot and *emits* light.

Information in sentence 2 tells us that a conductor lets electrons pass through easily. Sentence 4 explains that the filament does not easily allow electrons to flow through it. The evidence in these sentences together tell us that a flashlight bulb filament is not a good conductor.

Some questions in Science Detective ask you to find the sentence(s) that give the best evidence for your answer. To help you find a particular sentence, all the sentences in the lessons are numbered and paragraphs are lettered. Questions may ask you to give the numbers of sentences or the letters of paragraphs where you found answers.

You may have to go back and search the lesson for evidence to prove your answer is correct. All critical thinkers read carefully and then reread what they have read to make sure they understand what is explained. By reading carefully, they are sure they did not miss any important information or details. It is your mission to find the best evidence for your answers to the questions. In this book, you are the detective; that is why this book is called *Science Detective*™.

Science Detective Certificate

Awarded to

_____

for _____

Signed _____

Date _____

Unit I
PHYSICAL SCIENCE

1—Observable Physical Properties of Objects & Materials

A [1]Have you ever seen the color of a snowflake? [2]Have you felt the softness of a pillow or the roughness of sandpaper? [3]These qualities that describe objects or materials are their **properties**.

B [4]Physical properties are properties that we can easily **observe** with our **senses**—by seeing, hearing, touching, or smelling. [5]Color, hardness, texture, size, shape, and smell are physical properties.

C [6]Physical properties are helpful when we need to identify substances. [7]Sometimes two different substances can appear the same until we observe them more closely. [8]For example, both salt and sugar are white, are made up of small crystals, and look powdery. [9]You might not be able to tell them apart by just looking, though. [10]A piece of brown plastic might look just like a piece of chocolate. [11]However, they melt at different temperatures. [12]If you hold them in your hand awhile, you'll see which is the real chocolate by the mess it makes!

D [13]The temperature at which a substance starts changing from solid to liquid is its **melting point**. [14]When a substance boils, it is at its **boiling point**. [15]The melting point and the boiling point are physical properties of a substance. [16]Some melting and boiling points are listed below.

Melting Points		Boiling Points	
salt	800°	water	100°
sugar	450°	alchohol	80°
ice	0°	mercury	350°

800° means 800 degrees. Degrees are given in Celsius, described in the next lesson.

Mercury is the liquid used in thermometers.

E [17]Melting points, boiling points, and other kinds of information can be displayed by using a **bar graph**. [18]This type of diagram is often used by scientists to compare information. [19]The graph below allows you to compare the hardness of three substances.

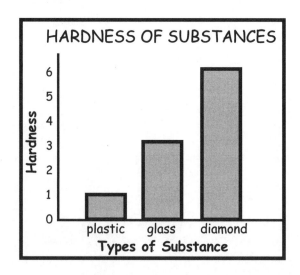

HARDNESS OF SUBSTANCES

1. For each statement, circle T or F for true or false. In each blank, write the letter of the PARAGRAPH that gives the best evidence for your answer.

    a. An object's size is a physical property.   T F __

    b. Physical properties are difficult to see.   T F __

    c. Bar graphs are rarely used in science.   T F __

2. Which of the following conclusions does the *Hardness of Substances* graph support? Circle Yes or No for each.

    a. Glass is harder than plastic.

        Yes   No

    b. Glass could scratch a diamond.

        Yes   No

    c. Plastic is harder than rubber.

        Yes   No

3. What is the increase in temperature from the time ice melts until it boils?

    a. 100 degrees   c. 800 degrees

    b. 450 degrees   d. 0 degrees

4. What is the most likely meaning of *observe*, as it is used in sentence 4?

    a. figure out   c. explain

    b. notice   d. ignore

5. Look at the bar graph below, and then answer the question.

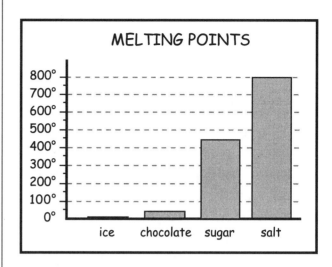

What is the difference between the melting points of chocolate and sugar?

a. 100 degrees   c. 400 degrees

b. 250 degrees   d. 700 degrees

6. Complete the bar graph below. Write the labels *mercury* and *alcohol* under the bars showing their boiling points. Above the *water* label, draw a bar to show the boiling point of water.

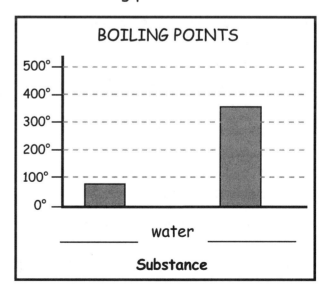

2—Measuring Physical Properties

A [1]Before you dress for school, you need only know whether it is very cold or hot outside. [2]But in science, it is important to know the *exact* temperature.

B [3]When you measure carefully to get exact information, you are being accurate. [4]**Accuracy** is making careful measurements that are exactly correct. [5]How could you be more accurate about describing the temperature outside? [6]You might look at a thermometer and read the numbers giving the exact temperature.

C [7]**Temperature** is a measure of how hot or cold an object is. [8]When you use a thermometer to find how hot or cold something is, you are measuring a physical property. [9]Therefore, the temperature of the air outside is a physical property. [10]**Measuring** is using a tool to accurately describe a physical property—for example, using a thermometer to measure temperature.

D [11]Can you name other physical properties and the tools that are used to measure them? [12]You already know that you can measure weight using a bathroom scale. [13]The length of an object can be measured using a ruler. [14]When making a cake, you would need to measure how much space flour takes up—its *volume*.

E [15]Saying that something has a big or small size is not an accurate way to describe it. [16]To be accurate, you must use a tool like a **metric ruler**, shown below. [17]A metric ruler accurately measures short distances like the width of a coin or the length of a paper clip.

F [18]A **thermometer** is a tool that accurately measures temperature. [19]It is made of a hollow glass or plastic tube. [20]At the bottom of the tube is a bulb filled with a red liquid. [21]When the liquid gets warmer, it takes up more space. [22]So as the liquid heats up, it climbs the hollow tube. [23]As it cools down, it takes less space and goes lower.

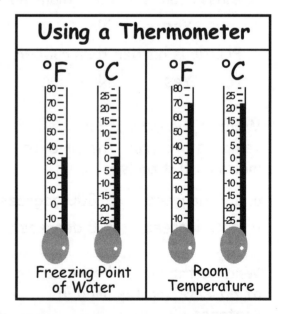

G [24]The unit used to measure temperature is the *degree*. [25]Its symbol is a small circle. [26]Notice that there are two different temperature scales. [27]One is the Fahrenheit (F) scale, and the other is the Celsius (C) scale.

1. For each statement, circle T or F for true or false. In the blanks, write the letter(s) of the <u>PARAGRAPH</u>(s)that give the best evidence for your answer.

    a. An accurate measurement is a correct measurement.

    T F ____

    b. Students need to know the exact outside temperature before dressing for school.

    T F ____

    c. Weight is measured with a ruler.   T F ____ , ____

2. Room temperature is about

    a. 0° F.   c. 22° F.

    b. 22° C.   d. 15° C.

3. If you need two cups of sugar to make cookies, what physical property will you measure?

    a. volume   c. temperature

    b. height   d. weight

    Which sentence provides the best evidence for your answer?
    ____

4. Write the abbreviation for each kind of temperature scale.
    Fahrenheit ____   Celsius ____

    It is 32° C outside. It is probably which season? (Use the thermometers in the lesson to see what 32° Celsius equals in Fahrenheit degrees.)

        winter   summer

5. Place each coin on the metric ruler and measure its length. (You may round to the nearest 1/2 cm.)

    a. dime   ____ cm
    b. nickel   ____ cm
    c. quarter   ____ cm

6. The difference in size between a dime and a quarter is ____ the difference between a dime and a nickel.

    a. the same as
    b. larger than
    c. smaller than

°C

For questions 7 and 8, see *Using a Thermometer* in the lesson.

7. On the thermometer at the right, circle the Celsius temperature that is the same as 32° Fahrenheit. Label it "F."

8. On the thermometer at the right, draw a box around the Celsius temperature that is the same as room temperature. Label it "R."

9. True or false: Thermometers use liquids that take up less space as they get warmer.

    T   F

    Which sentence provides the best evidence for your answer?
    ____

3—Classification of Matter

A [1]Imagine trying to find a book in a library if the thousands of books were not organized into topics. [2]It would be difficult! [3]Could you find a book about baseball in a library that did not have a section called sports? [4]You would have to search through all the books until you found the one you were looking for. [5]It might take weeks! [6]To make it easy to find what you want, libraries organize books with similar topics together.

B [7]A **classification system** is used to *organize* things or ideas so that they are easy to find or use. [8]Classification systems are made up of categories. [9]A **category** is a group of things that have a lot in common. [10]Once the system has been created, any new thing or idea can be easily put in the right place.

C [11]Classification systems are used all the time to help scientists organize information and ideas. [12]For example, they organize information about matter. [13]**Matter** is anything that takes up space and has mass. [14]**Mass** means how much stuff an object is made of. [15]Scientists classify matter into three categories: solid, liquid, and gas.

D [16]Scientists also classify matter as either a metal or a nonmetal. [17]If a material is shiny and hard, it is considered a metal. [18]If it is not shiny and is soft, it is a nonmetal. [19]Wood and chalk are nonmetals; iron and silver are metals.

E [20]Often, it is helpful to make a diagram of a classification system.

[21]This makes it easier to see how categories are connected to each other. [22]A **classification chart** shows how categories are organized in a classification system.

F [23]For example, think about the way a grocery store organizes what it sells into categories. [24]Can you think of examples to put in each food category below?

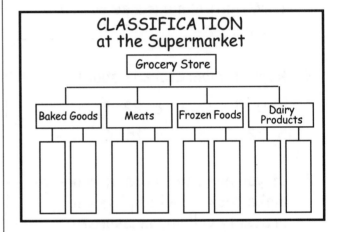

CLASSIFICATION at the Supermarket

G [25]Below is a chart showing how a scientist might classify different forms of matter into categories. [26]Can you think of examples of solids, liquids, and gases that belong in the categories of the chart below?

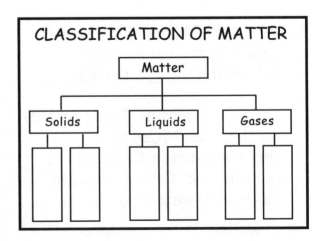

CLASSIFICATION OF MATTER

1. For each statement, circle T or F for true or false. In each blank, write the number of the <u>SENTENCE</u> that gives the best evidence for your answer.

   a. You are likely to find a book about the basketball player Michael Jordan in the science section of the library. T F ___

   b. A classification system can help organize foods into similar groups.   T F ___

   c. Solids, liquids, and gases belong to a group called *matter*.

                              T F ___

   d. Matter is anything that takes up space and has mass. T F ___

2. The oxygen that we breathe can be classified in which group of matter?

   a. metals   c. gases

   b. solids   d. liquids

3. What is the most likely meaning of *organize* as it is used in sentence 7?

   a. recycle   c. throw out

   b. put in order   d. put together

4. Look at the classification chart below. Think about sports that you have seen or played. Finish filling in the chart.

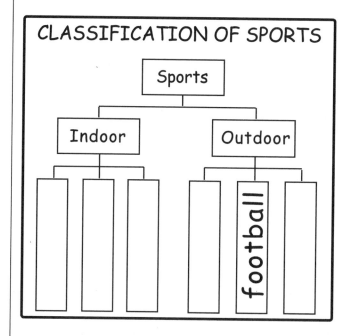

5. Think about the differences between metals and nonmetals, and then finish filling in the chart below. Use paragraph D to help you.

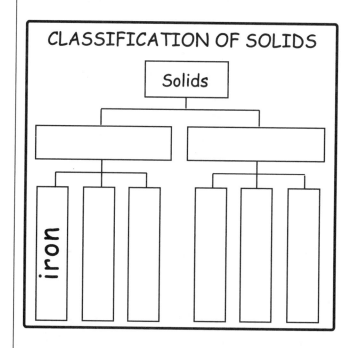

4—States of Matter

A [1]For many years, people did not know what matter was made of. [2]The ancient Greeks tried to figure out what would happen if a rock were broken into smaller and smaller pieces.

B [3]They predicted that you would get to a point where you could not break it down further. [4]You would be left with tiny particles. [5]They would be so small that you would not be able to see them with your eyes. [6]They called these particles *atoms*. [7]An **atom** is the building block of all matter.

C [8]Matter can be classified into three states: solid, liquid, or gas. [9]In the **solid state**, atoms are tightly packed and move very little; they vibrate but stay in one place. [10]In the **liquid state**, atoms can move enough to slide past each other. [11]In the **gas state**, atoms are free from one another and move quickly, so they are farther apart.

D [12]The states of matter can be described by *shape*. [13]Think of brick, water, and air as examples of matter in the three states. [14]In which state does matter always keep the same shape? [15]In which states can the shape change?

E [16]The states of matter can also be described in terms of **volume**. [17]Volume is the amount of space an object takes up. [18]Do you think the volume of a solid is constant? [19](If you move a brick, will its volume change?) [20]How about gas in a balloon after it is heated so the atoms move far apart? [21]Does the volume of gas change?

F [22]To easily understand information, we can organize it in a table. [23]For example, the table below makes it easy to compare information about utility vehicles. [24]See if you can tell which vehicle costs the most money. [25]Which gets the best gas mileage? [26]Which would be the best choice for a large family?

Utility Vehicles			
	Miles per Gallon (fuel)	Number of Passengers	Price of Vehicle
Pickup Truck	17	3	$25,000
Minivan	20	7	$30,000
SUV	12	5	$35,000

G [27]Tables are very useful for organizing information—maybe that's why science textbooks are filled with them! [28]Tables make it easy to learn by comparing. [29]The table below arranges information about solids, liquids, and gases. [30]Look at the table and think about the following questions. [31]Does a solid have a definite shape? [32]Do atoms of gas move slowly or quickly?

States of Matter			
	Movement of Atoms	Definite Shape?	Definite Volume?
Solid	vibration	yes	yes
Liquid	slow	no	yes
Gas	quick	no	no

1. For each statement, circle T or F for true or false. In each blank, write the number of the <u>SENTENCE</u> that gives the best evidence for your answer.

   a. All things are made of atoms.
      T F _____

   b. Metal is one of the three states of matter.
      T F _____

   c. In a gas, atoms stay together in one place.
      T F _____

2. When ice melts, it changes into water. It goes from a solid state into a liquid state. Describe what happens to the motion of the atoms when ice melts.

   _____

   _____

   _____

   Write the numbers of the two sentences that give the best evidence for your answer. _____,

   _____

3. What is the most likely meaning of the word *particles*, as it is used in sentence 6?

   a. large pieces   c. the whole thing
   b. rocks   d. small pieces

4. Use the information in the *Utility Vehicles* table in the lesson to complete the following chart. In each blank cell, write PT (for Pickup Truck), MV (for Minivan), or SUV. (Remember: it is best to have the most room and the least cost!)

Utility Vehicles			
	Miles per Gallon (fuel)	Number of Passengers	Price of Vehicles
Best			
Worst			

5. Complete the table below. Show how the atoms might be spaced apart in a liquid and in a gas (atoms of a solid are drawn for you).

   Also, describe the speed of movement of atoms in a solid and in a liquid (the movement of gas is described for you).

States of Matter		
State	Spacing of atoms	Movement of atoms
solid	 ⭕⭕⭕⭕ ⭕⭕⭕⭕ ⭕⭕⭕⭕	
liquid		
gas		quick

5—Change of Phase

A [1]Rub your hands together quickly for 10 seconds then hold them to your face. [2]Notice how warm your palms feel. [3]When you rubbed your hands, you created *friction*. [4]Friction produces **heat**, a form of energy.

B [5]It took muscle energy to move your hands. [6]Was the muscle energy changed into heat energy when you rubbed your palms together?

C [7]When you rub your hands together quickly, the atoms that make up your skin move faster. [8]As they do, they produce friction, and friction produces heat. [9]Therefore, your palms get warmer. [10]Heat can also come from other sources, such as fire, the sun, or an electric stove. [11]When heat from any source is applied to a substance, the atoms in that substance speed up and the substance gets warmer.

> You put a warm substance in the refrigerator. Is heat removed from the substance? What happens to the speed of the atoms?

D [12]The atoms of a solid normally move very little. [13]As you add more heat to a solid, its atoms move faster and faster. [14]When enough heat is added, the solid melts. [15]That means that when enough heat is *applied* to a solid, it changes state from a solid to a liquid. [16]This change in state from solid to liquid is called **melting**. [17]Think of a similar definition for *freezing*.

E [18]When there is a change in state because atoms have speeded up or slowed down, scientists say that there has been a **change in phase.**

F [19]Now think about liquids. [20]If enough heat energy is applied to a liquid, it will become a gas. [21]As water is heated, it gets hotter and hotter until it boils. [22]A gas called water vapor is produced. [23]If the water is left to boil long enough, all the water will vaporize. [24]**Vaporization** is the change in phase from a liquid to a gas.

G [25]Sometimes a gas will lose heat and return to liquid. [26]Think of a hot shower. [27]The hot water produces a lot of water vapor. [28]You may have seen what happens when hot water vapor touches a cold surface like a bathroom mirror! [29]The vapor cools and changes into a liquid. [30]The change in phase from a gas to a liquid is called **condensation**.

H [31]A **line graph** shows how one thing affects another over a period of time. [32]The line graph below shows what happens when you deposit 5 dollars a month in a savings account. [33]Think about how much money you save as time goes by. [34]How much money do you save in 3 months?

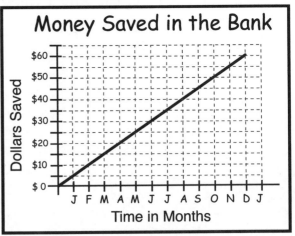

Money Saved in the Bank

Dollars Saved

$60
$50
$40
$30
$20
$10
$0

J F M A M J J A S O N D J

Time in Months

1. For each statement, circle T or F for true or false. In the blanks, write the letter(s) of the PARAGRAPH(s)that give the best evidence for your answer.

   a. Friction produces energy.

   T F ____

   b. Cooling an object speeds up its atoms.   T F ____, ____

   c. A solid can become a liquid by slowing its atoms.   T F ____

   d. A vapor is a gas.   T F ____

2. Look again at the graph called *Money Saved in the Bank*. How much money has been saved after 1 year and 1 month? (Hint: use a ruler to continue the line.) _____

3. What is the most likely meaning of *applied to,* as used in sentence 15?

   a. taken off   c. removed from

   b. made into   d. added to

   Write the number of the sentence that gives the best evidence for your answer. _____

4. Does it take energy to change liquid water into water vapor? ____
   Write the letter of the paragraph that best supports your answer. ____

5. Based on paragraph D, what is a likely definition for *freezing*?

   _____

   _____

   _____

Use the graph below to answer questions 6 and 7.

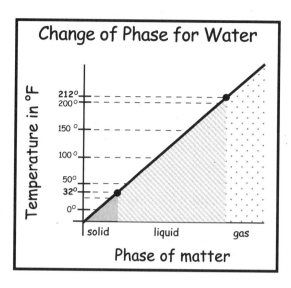

6. Which statement is supported by the graph? Water is

   a. a solid at 190° F.
   b. a gas at 190° F.
   c. a liquid at 190° F.
   d. a vapor at 0° F.

7. Look at the graph above. Water is in which phase of matter at the following temperatures?
   (S = solid, G = gas, L = liquid)
   a. 19° F _____   c. 230° F _____
   b. 90° F _____   d. 0° F _____

8. What could you do to a bathroom mirror to prevent it from fogging up during a hot shower?

   _____

   _____

   Write the letter of the paragraph that best supports your answer. ____

6—Position, Distance, and Motion

A [1]When you tell someone where an object is, you describe its position. [2]**Position** is the exact *location* of an object. [3]Think about lost treasure. [4]A treasure map describes the exact position of a treasure chest. [5]Knowing the object's position helps you find it easily.

B [6]If the position of an object has changed, the object has moved. [7]Motion describes the movement of an object from one place to another. [8]Therefore, **motion** is a change of position.

C [9]The measurement of how much an object's position has changed is **distance**. [10]Distance can also be the measurement from one object to another. [11]Think about the distance from your home to your school or the distance between your knee and your ankle. [12]Long distances are usually measured in kilometers or miles. [13]Short distances are usually measured in centimeters or inches.

D [14]Another measurement that involves distance and motion is speed. [15]We think of speed as how fast an object is moving. [16]If two cars are traveling from New York to Boston and one gets there before the other, one changed its position faster. [17]**Speed** is a measurement of distance traveled during a period of time. [18]Speed is measured in units of distance and time, for example in miles per hour.

Finding the Position of an Object

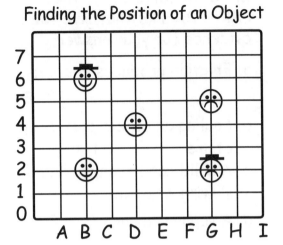

E [19]The diagram above shows the positions of happy and sad faces. [20]Each face is located at a place where a vertical line and a horizontal line cross each other. [21]A **vertical** line goes up and down. [22]A **horizontal** line goes left and right. [23]Look at the happy face wearing a hat. [24]Two lines are passing through it. [25]One line is vertical. [26]The other line is horizontal.

F [27]Find the number of the horizontal line going through the happy face wearing a hat. [28]Find the letter of the vertical line. [29]The position of the happy face wearing a hat is at the point where line B and line 6 cross each other. [30]In other words, the happy face wearing a hat is at B6. [31]What is the position of the sad face wearing a hat?

G [32]A diagram that uses vertical and horizontal lines to show a position is called a **grid**. [33]Grids can be labeled with letters or numbers or both. [34]The letters and numbers used to tell the exact position of an object on a grid are called the **coordinates**.

1. For each statement, circle T or F for true or false. In the blanks, write the number(s) of the <u>SENTENCE</u>(s) that give the best evidence for your answer.

   a. Time is a part of speed.

   T F ___, ___

   b. Things can change position without moving.   T F ___

   c. Scientists use the word *distance* to mean movement from one place to another.

   T F ___

2. Look at the grid in the lesson. Write the coordinates of each object next to its description. The first one is done for you.

   a. Sad face with no hat   <u>G 5</u>

   b. Happy face with no hat   ___ ___

   c. Face with no expression ___ ___

   d. Sad face with a hat   ___ ___

3. What is the most likely meaning of the word *location*, as it is used in sentence 2?

   a. motion
   b. objects
   c. certain place
   d. passage of time

4. Look at the grid in the lesson. Find a point exactly between the two happy faces. What are the coordinates of that point? ___ ___

5. On the grid below, draw the faces listed at the coordinates given.

   a. ☺ at B2
   b. ☹ at G5
   c. 😐 at E4
   d. 😀 at H3

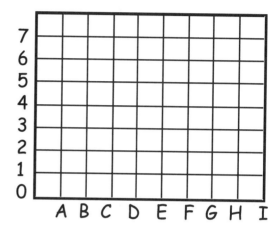

6. The map below uses coordinates to help find cities. Next to each city, write the correct letter and number coordinates.

   a. Miami, FL   ___ ___
   b. Los Angeles, CA*   ___ ___
   c. San Francisco, CA ___ ___
   d. Chicago, IL   ___ ___

   *southern California

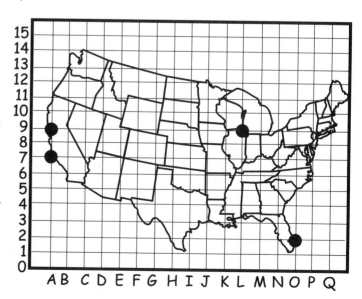

7—Pushing and Pulling Forces

A ¹Think about how you would move a wagon up a hill. ²A wagon will not move by itself. ³You must either push or pull it to change its position. ⁴In science, a push or a pull is called a **force**.

B ⁵Force is needed to start an object moving. ⁶Force is also needed to stop an object. ⁷For example, to move a bicycle you must push down on its pedals. ⁸To stop the bike, you must put pressure on the brakes. ⁹Forces start and stop a bicycle.

C ¹⁰Forces are needed not only to start and stop an object's motion. ¹¹They are also needed to change the motion of an object that is already moving. ¹²Whenever you steer your bicycle, you are applying a force to its handlebars.

D ¹³Sometimes the force that makes an object move cannot be seen. ¹⁴Think of an iron nail and a magnet. ¹⁵When the magnet gets close to the nail, they attract each other. ¹⁶Do you see any force pushing or pulling the nail? ¹⁷No, because the force produced by a magnet is invisible. ¹⁸This invisible force that pulls on metal objects is called **magnetism**.

E ¹⁹What about other invisible forces? ²⁰Think of an apple falling from a tree. ²¹You can't see any forces pushing or pulling it down, can you? ²²**Gravity** is the invisible force that pulls objects down toward the earth.

F ²³The force of gravity pulling on an object is **weight**. ²⁴The weight of an object is given in pounds or in

Newtons. ²⁵Weight is measured with a **scale**.

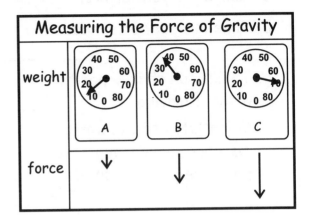

Measuring the Force of Gravity

G ²⁶Look at the diagram above. ²⁷How much do you think each object weighs? ²⁸Notice how the arrows change. ²⁹The length of the arrow is related to the object's weight. ³⁰Scientists often use arrows to represent forces. ³¹An arrow that shows a force is called a **vector.**

H ³²The diagram below compares some familiar forces. ³³Can you name other examples of forces?

Comparing Forces

	small force	large force
pedaling a bicycle	→ flat road	→ uphill
hitting a baseball	→ bunt	→ home run
the wind blowing	→ breeze	→ hurricane

1. For each statement, circle T or F for true or false. In the blanks, write the number(s) of the SENTENCE(s) that give the best evidence for your answer.

   a. Pulling a sled is an example of a force.　T　F ___

   b. A steel pin falling to a magnet below it is being pulled by only one force.　T　F ___ , ___

   c. The longer the vector, the larger the force.　T　F ___

2. Is each conclusion supported by the *Comparing Forces* diagram in the lesson? In each blank, write Y or N for yes or no.

   a. Pedaling uphill takes more force than pedaling on flat land.　___

   b. Wind is invisible.　___

   c. Below, force A is greater than force B.　___

   $\longrightarrow \quad \longrightarrow$
   　A　　　B

3. Which vector shows the force of gravity? (See the *Measuring the Force of Gravity* chart.)

   a. $\longrightarrow$　　　c. $\downarrow$

   b. $\longleftarrow$　　　d. $\uparrow$

   Write the number of the sentence in paragraph E that gives the best evidence for your answer. ___

4. Complete the diagram below. Draw vectors to show force for A and C, and draw an arrow to show weight on the scale for B.

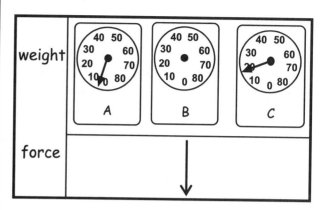

5. Fill in the blanks in the diagram below. Be sure to include vectors that represent the forces you select (the first one is drawn for you).

	small force	large force
using a hammer	$\longrightarrow$ tapping	
	ripple	tidal wave
sounds		scream

6. Think about how a driver slows down a car. Describe the force that slows the car and why it works.

   _____

   _____

   Write the letter of the paragraph that gives the best evidence for your answer. ___

8—Sound, Hearing, and Force

A [1]You know that forces are produced by pushing or pulling. [2]Did you know that forces can produce sound?

B [3]A **vibration** is a back-and-forth motion. [4]Objects vibrate when they move very quickly back and forth. [5]Stretch a rubber band between your thumb and index finger. [6]Pull back one side of the loop, and let go. [7]How would you describe the motion of the rubber band after you release it? [8]Does it vibrate?

C [9]Whenever an object vibrates, it pushes the air around it. [10]If the object vibrates slowly, it will push the air around it slowly. [11]If it vibrates quickly, it will push the air around it quickly.

D [12]A vibrating guitar string makes air particles vibrate. [13]The vibrations form air waves, which reach your ear. [14]The ear is a machine that changes the vibrating air waves into electrical signals. [15]The electrical signals travel to the brain, where they are *converted* into sounds you hear. [16]**Sound** is the way the brain understands vibrations entering the ear. [17]Sound is not the vibrating guitar string, the vibrating air, or the vibrating inner ear. [18]**Hearing** is the series of actions by which vibrating forces are received by the ear and understood by the brain.

E [19]A series of actions that happen in order is called a **process**. [20]For example, getting ready for school or work each day is a process. [21]A **flow chart** is a diagram that makes it easier to understand the steps in a process.

THE PROCESS OF GETTING READY FOR THE DAY

wake up → brush teeth → get dressed → eat breakfast

F [22]Look at the diagram above. [23]It is a flow chart showing the steps you might go through in the morning. [24]Would it make any sense to reverse the order of the steps?

G [25]Another term for steps that are taken in a particular order is **sequence**. [26]You follow a sequence of steps when you get up in the morning.

H [27]Hearing is a process that follows a sequence of steps. [28]The first step is an object that vibrates. [29]The last step is a sound being heard. [30]What are the steps in between?

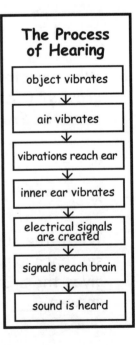

The Process of Hearing

object vibrates
↓
air vibrates
↓
vibrations reach ear
↓
inner ear vibrates
↓
electrical signals are created
↓
signals reach brain
↓
sound is heard

1. For each statement, circle T or F for true or false. In each blank, write the letter of the <u>PARAGRAPH</u> that gives the best evidence for your answer.

   a. Sound depends on vibrations.
                                    T F ____

   b. Hearing occurs within a vibrating object.   T F ____

   c. The ear can make electrical signals.   T F ____

2. For each conclusion below, decide if it is supported by the *Process of Hearing* flow chart in the lesson. In each blank, write Y or N for yes or no.

   a. Vibrating air causes the inner ear to vibrate.   ____

   b. The process of hearing follows a sequence of steps.   ____

   c. Sounds are heard in the brain.   ____

   d. Electrical signals make the inner ear vibrate.   ____

3. In sentence 15, the word *converted* most likely means

   a. heard.
   b. changed.
   c. stretched.
   d. vibrated.

4. Normally, we hear sounds when air particles vibrate against the ear. If you hear sounds under water, it is probably because

   a. air particles are vibrating over your head.

   b. water particles are vibrating against your ear.

   c. air is coming out of your ears.

5. The following steps are out of order. Put the letters of the steps in the boxes of the flow chart to show the correct sequence as shown in the lesson.

   A. vibrations reach ear
   B. electrical signals are made
   C. sound is heard
   D. air vibrates
   E. object vibrates
   F. signals reach brain
   G. inner ear vibrates

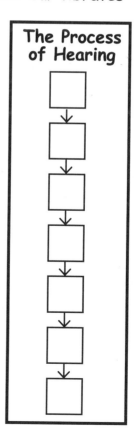

The Process of Hearing

9—Characteristics of Sound

A [1]Sounds are caused by objects that vibrate. [2]As an object vibrates, it pushes against surrounding air particles. [3]Vibrations spread out and away from the object as sound waves.

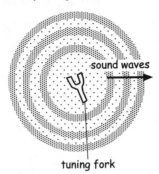

sound waves

tuning fork

B [4]Each vibration forces air particles closer together and then farther apart. [5]The diagram at the right shows these areas of packed and loose air particles. [6]Areas of tightly packed air particles are called **compressions**.

Air particles pushed together by the force of a vibrating object

packed | loose | packed | loose | packed | loose

C [7]The faster an object vibrates, the more often air particles are pushed tightly together. [8]Objects that vibrate slowly produce fewer compressions than objects that vibrate quickly. [9]It is the number of compressions reaching your ear every second that makes a sound high or low. [10]A slowly vibrating object, like a fog horn or a bass drum, produces low sounds. [11]A quickly vibrating object, like a whistle or a violin, produces high sounds.

D [12]A sound's **tone** is how high or low the sound is. [13]If a great number of compressions reach the ear each second, does the sound have a high or low tone? [14]That's right, it's a high tone.

E [15]Besides tone, in what ways can sounds be different? [16]Sounds can be very soft like a whisper or very loud like a scream. [17]What makes a sound loud or soft? [18]The force of air hitting the eardrum in your middle ear produces sound. [19]The greater the force, the louder the sound. [20]The loudness of a sound is its **volume**.

F [21]The diagram below shows the three sections of the human ear. [22]The outer ear takes in sound compressions as air beats against the eardrum. [23]The middle ear changes sound compressions into electrical signals. [24]The inner ear *transfers* these electrical signals to a nerve that connects to the brain. [25]Sound is heard only after the brain receives electrical signals from the inner ear. [26]The brain turns these signals into the sounds we hear.

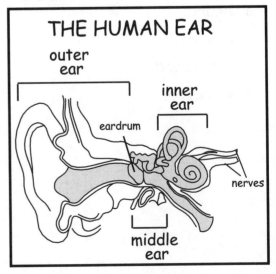

THE HUMAN EAR

outer ear

inner ear

eardrum

nerves

middle ear

1. For each statement, circle T or F for true or false. In each blank, write the letter of the <u>PARAGRAPH</u> that gives the best evidence for your answer.

   a. A squeaky wheel is an example of a low tone.   T F ____

   b. Sounds are heard after an object vibrates.   T F ____

   c. The greater the amount of air moved by a vibrating object, the louder the sound. T F ____

   d. The vocal cords of a bear vibrate faster than the vocal cords of a mouse. T F ____

2. Write the letter of the diagram below that could show each sound described.

   a. the higher tone   ____

   b. the sound of a ship's horn ____

   c. the sound of a whistle   ____

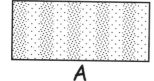   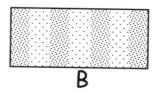

   A   B

3. Imagine that you could see the air particles compressed by a whistle and the air particles compressed by a vibrating tuba. Use complete sentences to tell how they would look different.

   _____

   _____

   _____

4. Imagine the roar of a lion and the squeak of a mouse. Use the words *tone* and *volume* to describe the differences between the two sounds. Fill in the rest of the chart to help you.

	Tone	Volume
Lion	Low	
Mouse		

   _____

   _____

   _____

5. Which part of a telephone carries electrical signals like a nerve?

   a. earpiece

   b. mouthpiece

   c. telephone cord

   d. telephone dialer

6. In sentence 24, what is the most likely meaning of the word *transfers*?

   a. changes

   b. slows down

   c. sends

   d. attaches

7. If you tighten a guitar string, it will sound higher when played. Use a complete sentence to tell what the string does that causes the sound to change.

   _____

   _____

   _____

10—Characteristics of Light: Reflection and Refraction

A ¹**Energy** is necessary to make anything happen. ²We do not hear sounds unless air particles are packed together using the energy of a vibrating object. ³So, hearing uses energy. ⁴Without energy, there is no sound.

B ⁵Seeing also depends on energy. ⁶What we see is created in the brain by light energy reaching the eye. ⁷Without light, *images* cannot be seen. ⁸Therefore, vision, like hearing, depends on energy.

C ⁹**Light** is a form of energy. ¹⁰Light normally travels in a straight line. ¹¹Think about using a flashlight at night. ¹²The beam of light does not bend around corners. ¹³Think about making shadow figures with your hands on a wall. ¹⁴If the light were to bend around your hand, there would be no shadow.

D ¹⁵Where does light come from? ¹⁶Light comes from many places. ¹⁷For example, fire, lightning, and light bulbs produce light. ¹⁸In all cases, energy is needed to create light.

E ¹⁹Scientists call a beam, or thin line of light, a **ray**. ²⁰Rays of light are drawn as thin straight lines, usually with arrowheads.

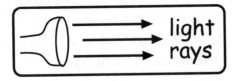

light rays

F ²¹When a ray of light hits an object, the light ray can do one of three things:

1) bounce off the object,
2) pass through the object unchanged, or
3) be changed by the object.

G ²²The bouncing of light rays off an object is called **reflection**. ²³If you shine a flashlight on a mirror, you will see the light beam reflect off the mirror by going in a different direction.

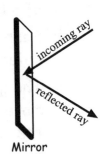

incoming ray
reflected ray
Mirror

H ²⁴A ray of light could pass through an object unchanged. ²⁵Light can pass directly through a glass window.

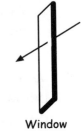

Window

I ²⁶Finally, when a light ray hits an object, the ray could be changed. ²⁷For example, put a pencil in a half glass of water and observe it through the side of the glass. ²⁸The *distorted* image of the pencil is an example of refraction. ²⁹**Refraction** is the bending of light as it passes from one material to another. ³⁰In this example, light is bent as it passes through glass and water.

J ³¹Refraction is a useful property of matter. ³²A **lens** is a tool that takes advantage of this property. ³³Lenses bend light. ³⁴We use lenses in telescopes, microscopes, and eyeglasses to see more and to see more clearly.

1. For each statement, circle T or F for true or false. In the blanks, write the letter(s) of the <u>PARAGRAPH</u>(s) that give the best evidence for your answer.

   a. Vision requires energy. T F ____

   b. Shadows are created by bending light rays.   T F ____

   c. Your image in a mirror is an example of refracted light.
      T F ____, ____

   d. Lenses depend on reflected light to make an image bigger.
      T F ____

2. A pencil whose image is *distorted*, as described in sentence 28, probably looks

   a. broken.

   b. unchanged.

   c. straight.

   d. yellow.

3. Is it reasonable to conclude that smelling takes energy? _____ Use complete sentences to explain your answer.

   _____

   _____

   _____

   Write the letters of the two paragraphs that give the best evidence for your answer.

   ____, ____

4. Which statements are supported by evidence you have read in the lesson? Circle the letters of all correct answers.

   a. Light moving from the air into the ocean is probably bent.

   b. Light rays never change direction.

   c. Light rays are refracted after they hit a chalkboard.

   d. The directions of reflected rays is different from the direction of incoming rays.

5. Beside each statement, write the number of the picture it describes.

   a. Refraction   _____

   b. Reflection   _____

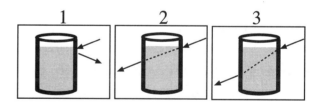

6. Explain why a pencil sitting partly in water looks the way it does. Use complete sentences.

   _____

   _____

   _____

7. As used in sentence 7, *images* probably means things that you can

   a. touch.   c. hear.

   b. see.   d. smell.

11—Heat, Sources of Heat, and Heat Conduction

A [1]**Heat** is the flow of energy from one object to another. [2]When matter changes from one phase to another, heat is added or taken away. [3]To boil water, heat energy must be added. [4]To freeze water, heat energy must be removed.

B [5]Think about what heat does. [6]When heat flows, it makes things warmer. [7]Heat flows in one direction only: from a warmer object to a cooler object.

C [8]Heat energy makes atoms vibrate faster. [9]The atoms in a hot object vibrate much faster than the atoms in a cool object. [10]When heat is added to a cool object, its atoms begin to vibrate faster and it gets warmer. [11]Heat is the flow of energy that makes atoms vibrate faster.

D [12]Do you know where heat comes from? [13]Heat comes from the sun, fire, heaters, the center of the earth, and many other *sources*. [14]Even living organisms, like people, dogs, and plants, make heat.

E [15]If an object is a source of heat, its atoms must be vibrating fast. [16]For example, the atoms of a heated iron vibrate very quickly. [17]**Cooling** results from losing heat. [18]As heat flows away from an object, its atoms vibrate more and more slowly. [19]After a hot iron is unplugged, it cools down as its heat flows into the cool room air. [20]Do you think heat will flow from the iron to the air forever? [21]Why not?

F [22]Heat flows when a warmer object comes in contact with a cooler object. [23]Think about what happens when ice cubes come in contact with warm water. [24]The ice melts and the water gets cooler. [25]Heat has flowed from the warmer object to the cooler object. [26]The flow of heat between objects that are touching is called **conduction**.

G [27]**Temperature** is the measure of how hot or cold an object is. [28]In other words, temperature is a measure of how fast the atoms of an object are vibrating. [29]The faster atoms vibrate, the warmer the temperature of the object.

H [30]Look at the *Temperature of Objects* bar graph below. [31]What do the numbers along the left side tell you? [32]What is the temperature of the coolest object on the graph?

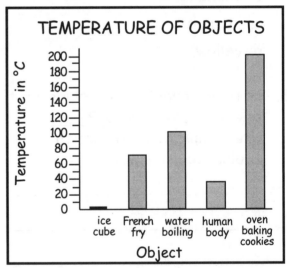

I [33]Remember what you have learned about heat. [34]Then look at the simple flow chart below. [35]Think about the purpose of the arrow and why it points from the sun to the earth instead of the other way.

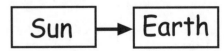

1. For each statement, circle T or F for true or false. In the blanks, write the number(s) of the <u>SENTENCE</u>(s) that give the best evidence for your answer.

   a. Atoms of hot and cold objects vibrate at the same speed.

      T F ____

   b. Heat flows from a cold floor to warm feet.   T F ____

   c. Temperature and heat are the same thing.   T F ____, ____

2. In sentence 13, the word *sources* probably means

   a. places in between.

   b. places things go to.

   c. places on fire.

   d. places things come from.

3. If the atoms of two snowballs are vibrating at the same speed, what can you conclude about their temperatures? Use one or more complete sentences to answer.

   _____

   _____

   _____

   _____

   Write the letter of the paragraph that gives the best evidence for your answer. ____

4. Finish the graph below by adding the correct labels and drawing the missing bar. Use the information in the table at the right.

Object	Tem-perature
hot tea	70°
candle flame	190°
ice cream	5°
summer day	30°

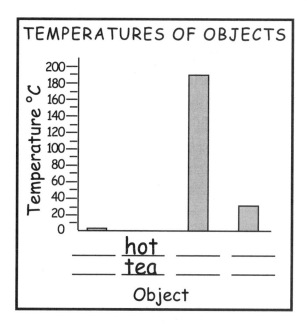

5. Finish writing names and drawing arrows to show the direction of heat flow between objects in each pair. Use these names: *Ice Cream, Fire, TV Dinner.*

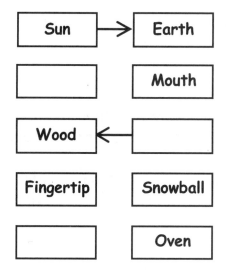

12—Electricity, Electrical Circuits, and Energy

A [1]Can you think of three different sources of energy that help to do work? [2]Your list probably includes heat from a stove or a fire. [3]You may also have listed wind or the burning of fuels like coal or gasoline. [4]Another source of useful energy is electricity.

B [5]**Electricity** is a form of energy that produces a force that can be used to do work. [6]Electricity is often used to make heat. [7]The heat is then used to do work. [8]Think of small particles moving through a wire. [9]These particles are called *electrons*. [10]The movement of electrons through a wire is used to make the heat produced by an electric stove.

C [11]The amount of work that can be done by electricity depends upon the number of electrons moving through a wire. [12]As more electrons move through the wire, more work can be done. [13]These electrons move through a wire like water moving through a pipe. [14]In fact, we say they form a *current*. [15]The thicker the wire, the greater the current it can carry. [16]The term **electric current** is used to describe the number of electrons moving through a wire every second. [17]A material that lets electrons pass through it easily is called a **conductor**.

D [18]If you have a source of electrons and a pathway for them to follow, you can do work. [19]Think about a flashlight. [20]What is the source of its electrons? [21]What kind of work do the electrons do when the flashlight is turned on?

E [22]When electrons flow through the flashlight bulb, they pass through a thin wire that is called a filament. [23]A filament is a poor conductor because it blocks, or *resists*, the flow of electrons. [24]As they are forced through the filament, they produce friction, and friction produces heat. [25]Forcing electrons through a filament produces so much heat that the wire gets white hot and *emits* light.

F [26]In order for electrons in the flashlight to do work, they must be able to flow from the battery to the bulb and back to the battery. [27]The pathway of a circular flow is called a circuit. [28]An **electric circuit** is the pathway through which an electric current flows.

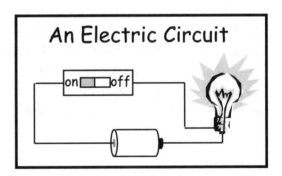

An Electric Circuit

G [29]The diagram above shows all the parts of an electric circuit in a flashlight. [30]The parts are

1) a source of electrons (battery),

2) a pathway (wire),

3) a *device* that does work (bulb), and

4) an on/off switch.

1. For each statement, circle T or F for true or false. In each blank, write the letter of the <u>PARAGRAPH</u> that gives the best evidence for your answer.

    a. Energy is used to do work.

        T F ____

    b. A thinner wire can carry more electric current than a thicker wire.   T F ____

    c. Electrons flowing through a good conductor produce more heat than electrons flowing through a poor conductor.

        T F ____

    d. Good conductors are used to make filaments.   T F ____

2. What is the most likely meaning of *emits*, as used in sentence 25?

    a. closes

    b. holds in

    c. opens up

    d. gives off

3. Electric current is measured in amperes (amps). One amp is the number of electrons that pass through a wire every second. Which of the following will require the thickest wire?

    a. 10 amp current

    b. 20 amp current

    c. 30 amp current

    d. 40 amp current

    Write the number of the sentence in paragraph C that gives the best evidence for your answer. ____

4. Two wires have the same electric current running through them. One wire is much hotter than the other. Can you conclude that the hotter wire resists the flow of electrons more?
    Use one or more complete sentences to explain your answer.

    _____

    _____

    _____

    Write the letter of the paragraph that gives the best evidence for your answer. ____

5. Draw a diagram showing a circuit with a battery, a switch, and three light bulbs. Use the diagram in the lesson to help you.

13—Symbols and Electric Circuits

A [1]A symbol is a letter or a picture that stands for something else. [2]In math, symbols are used all the time. [3]You probably know what each of the following math symbols stands for:

$$+ \quad - \quad x \quad \div \quad =$$

B [4]Symbols are also used to show important information quickly. [5]Some symbols give us information as we travel along a road. [6]Some symbols warn us of danger. [7]What does each symbol below mean?

C [8]Symbols are also used in science. [9]For example, elements, which make up all matter, are represented by letters. [10]O stands for oxygen, and N stands for nitrogen.

D [11]Symbols are used to simplify electrical diagrams. [12]Consider the diagram below of an electric circuit. [13]An electric circuit is made up of a source of electrons (battery), a path for them to follow (wire), a device* (such as a light bulb) that does some work, and an on/off switch.

* device: invention, machine, or gadget

E [14]Notice that each part of the electric circuit is represented by a sketch of the electrical part. [15]For example, the light bulb looks like a light bulb and the battery looks like a battery. [16]When electric circuits are simple and have few parts, using pictures of each part is *practical*. [17]However, when electric circuits are complicated, it takes too much work and too much space to use pictures. [18]Therefore, scientists have developed symbols to represent each electrical part. [19]Review the table of electrical symbols below.

Battery	⊣⊢
Wire	——
Switch (shown open)	⌐•/
Device (bulb)	/\/\/\

F [20]Look at the diagram below, and notice how little space the symbols take. [21]If we couldn't use symbols, imagine how much harder it would be to draw a circuit containing 12 batteries, 8 light bulbs, and 3 switches!

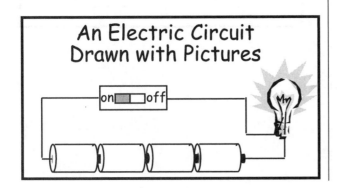

An Electric Circuit Drawn with Pictures

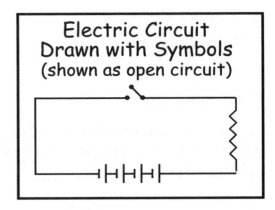

Electric Circuit Drawn with Symbols (shown as open circuit)

1. For each statement, circle T or F for true or false. In each blank, write the number of the <u>SENTENCE</u> that gives the best evidence for your answer.

   a. The symbol for the element sodium is a number.   T F ____

   b. An = sign is a symbol in math.   T F ____

   c. Symbols are used to save time.   T F ____

   d. Symbols make diagrams more complicated to create.   T F ____

2. What is the most likely meaning of *practical* as used in sentence 16?

   a. easy to do

   b. difficult

   c. hard to do

   d. confusing

3. Look at the circuit below. Complete it by drawing in the correct symbols for the switch, device, and battery.

4. Draw the symbol that could represent a radio (a device) in a circuit diagram.

5. Consider this switch: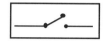

   a. Can an electric current flow through the switch in the open position shown?

                                    Yes   No

   b. Is this switch "on" or "off?"

                                    On   Off

   c. If a circuit is open when its switch is off, the circuit is _____ when its switch is on.

   d. Draw a symbol for a closed circuit.

6. Using symbols, draw a closed circuit that has a battery, a switch, and two devices. One of the devices should be an electric motor; show it with this symbol: Ⓜ

switch

device   battery

14—Magnets, Magnetism, and Electromagnetism

A [1]Remember that a force is a push or a pull—and forces are needed to do work. [2]Gravity and electricity are some familiar forces. [3]Magnetism is a force, too, and we'll explore it in this lesson. [4]If you have magnets and steel paper clips, you might want to get them out.

B [5]What is a magnetic force? [6]You can experience a magnetic force by holding a magnet near a piece of steel like a paper clip. [7]What happens? [8]The magnet pulls on the paper clip and moves it. [9]The magnet did work. [10]Therefore, a magnet produces force. [11]A **magnet** is a substance that attracts only objects that contain iron or steel. [12]A **magnetic force** is the force produced by a magnet.

C [13]A magnet attracts only the metal objects that are near it. [14]If you hold a magnet far enough away from a paper clip, it cannot move it. [15]The area around a magnet where magnetic forces can do work is called a **magnetic field**. [16]The stronger the magnet, the larger its magnetic field.

D [17]Most magnets have two ends. [18]Each end is called a pole. [19]A **pole** is the region of a magnet where it produces strong magnetic forces.

north pole	**magnet**	south pole

E [20]Look at the diagram of a *typical* magnet above. [21]Like most magnets, it has a north pole (N) and a south pole (S). [22]If you have two magnets and hold the opposite poles near each other (N to S), they will attract each other.

[23]If you hold the same poles near each other (N to N, or S to S), they will push away or *repel* each other.

F [24]Most magnets used to do work are created using electricity and are called **electromagnets**. [25]Electromagnets are made by passing an electric current through iron or steel. [26]Some typical electromagnetic devices are electric motors, doorbells, and buzzers. [27]Think how much work is done when an electromagnet is used in a junk yard to lift an automobile! [28]This graph shows how force and work are related.

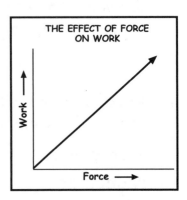

THE EFFECT OF FORCE ON WORK

Work

Force →

G [29]The graph below shows how the strength of an electromagnet is changed by the amount of electric current going through it. [30]Notice that the strength of an electromagnet increases as the electric current is increased. [31]If less magnetic force is produced, what could you conclude about the amount of electric current flowing through the magnet?

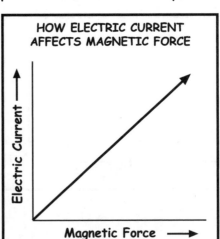

HOW ELECTRIC CURRENT AFFECTS MAGNETIC FORCE

Electric Current →

Magnetic Force →

1. For each statement, circle T or F for true or false. In the blanks, write the number(s) of the <u>SENTENCE</u>(s) that give the best evidence for your answer.

    a. Magnetism produces a force.

        T F ___, ___

    b. Work can be done without using a force.   T F ___, ___

    c. Steel and iron are attracted to a magnet.   T F ___

    d. As electric current increases, electromagnet strength decreases.   T F ___

2. What is the most likely meaning of *typical* as used in sentence 20?

    a. strange   c. unusual

    b. usual   d. large

3. Finish each sentence with the word *decreases* or *increases*.

    a. When the electric current <u>decreases</u>, the electromagnetic field

        _____.

    b. When the electric current <u>increases</u>, the electromagnetic field

        _____.

    c. When the electric current is <u>cut in half</u>, the electromagnetic field

        _____.

4. For each pair of magnets, predict the direction of movement. Draw an arrow beneath each magnet. The first has been done for you.

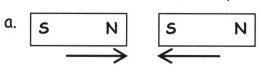

5. Complete the graph below by 1) labeling each arrow, and 2) adding a line to show the relationship. Read the statement below to help you.

> As electricity flows through an electromagnet, it produces a magnetic force. As the electric current increases, the magnetic force gets stronger.

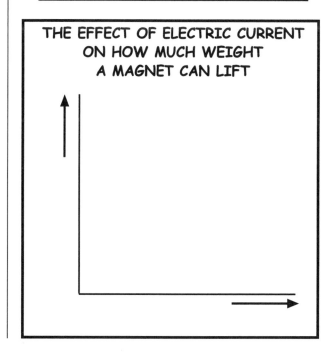

THE EFFECT OF ELECTRIC CURRENT
ON HOW MUCH WEIGHT
A MAGNET CAN LIFT

Unit II
LIFE SCIENCE

15—Animal and Plant Needs and the Environment

A [1]An **organism** is a living thing; people, ants, trees, flowers, and bacteria are organisms. [2]To live, all kinds of organisms must be able to grow and reproduce. [3]When an organism **reproduces**, it makes more of its own kind.

B [4]What else must organisms do to *survive*? [5]Organisms must be able to do work. [6]They must do work to get food. [7]They must do work to move. [8]What is necessary to do work? [9]Energy is necessary. [10]Remember, **energy** is the ability to do work. [11]Therefore, living things must be able to get energy to survive. [12]Where does a plant get its energy from? [13]Where do animals get energy from?

C [14]Living things need help from their environment to survive. [15]An **environment** is all the living and nonliving things that surround an organism. [16]Organisms need food, water, air, and a suitable climate. [17]What else does an organism need from its environment to survive? [18]Plants needs sunlight. [19]Animals need shelter.

D [20]Let's consider the squirrel. [21]To stay alive, a squirrel needs several things from its environment. [22]It needs food such as nuts and berries to eat, water to drink, air to breathe, and the shelter of a hollow tree trunk or other safe place to live.

E [23]Can an organism survive in an environment that does not have what it needs? [24]Of course not. [25]Think of a fish without water or a tree without sunlight!

F [26]Different environments contain different kinds of organisms. [27]A **desert** is very hot and dry, with almost no rain. [28]What kinds of organisms can survive in the desert? [29]Camels, cactus plants, snakes, buzzards, and some people can live there. [30]Can you think of organisms that could not live there?

G [31]Charts and tables can make information easier to understand. [32]For example, the classification chart below shows some of the organisms that can survive in a tropical rain forest.

ORGANISMS FOUND IN A TROPICAL RAIN FOREST ENVIRONMENT

```
              Rain Forest
    ┌──────────────┼──────────────┐
  snakes      palm trees        parrots
        monkeys        mosquitoes
```

H [33]A **table** is a chart that places information in columns so you can compare things. [34]The table below compares some needs of a bumble bee and a grizzly bear.

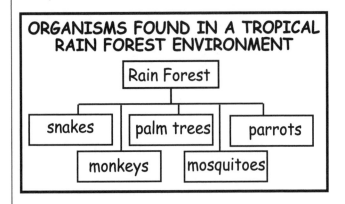

SURVIVAL NEEDS OF ANIMALS			
	Food	Shelter	Climate
Bumble bee	nectar	hive	warm
Grizzly bear	fish	den	cool

1. For each statement, circle T or F for true or false. In each blank, write the number of the <u>SENTENCE</u> that gives the best evidence for your answer.

   a. To continue to live, all types of organisms reproduce and grow.
      T F ___

   b. All organisms do work.
      T F ___

   c. Organisms do not need a source of energy.   T F ___

   d. Trees, bushes, logs, and grass are all organisms.   T F ___

2. What is the most likely meaning of *survive* as it is used in sentence 4?

   a. move around

   b. die

   c. continue to live

   d. stay in one place

3. Complete the classification chart below.

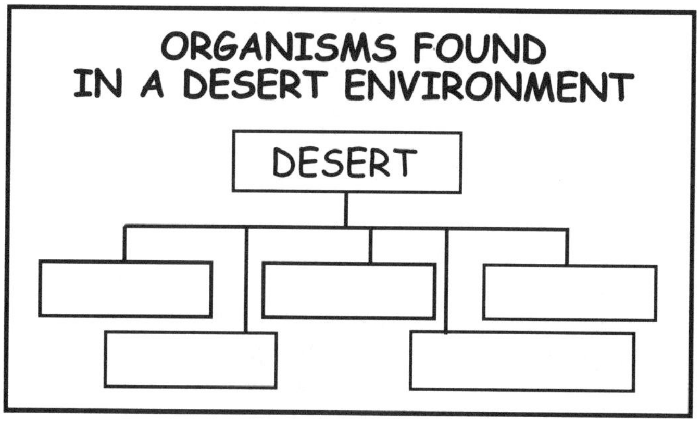

```
┌─────────────────────────────────┐
│    ORGANISMS FOUND               │
│  IN A DESERT ENVIRONMENT         │
│        ┌──────────┐              │
│        │ DESERT   │              │
│        └──────────┘              │
│     ┌────┐  ┌────┐  ┌────┐       │
│     │    │  │    │  │    │       │
│     └────┘  └────┘  └────┘       │
│        ┌────┐  ┌────┐            │
│        │    │  │    │            │
│        └────┘  └────┘            │
└─────────────────────────────────┘
```

4. Complete the table below for an eagle, seal, and spider by adding these words in the correct places: *eagle, spider, shelter, climate, mice, insects, fish, tree, web, ocean, cold, cool, warm.*

SURVIVAL NEEDS OF ORGANISMS			
	Food		
Seal			

5. Living things need help from their environment to survive. Write a sentence that gives examples of what an organism, such as a rabbit, needs to survive.

   _____

   _____

   _____

   Write the letter of the paragraph that best supports your answer. ___

6. Why are very few organisms found at the South Pole?

   _____

   _____

   _____

7. Why are so many different organisms found in the tropical rain forest?

   _____

   _____

   _____

16—Environments, Ecosystems, and Organisms

A [1]You have learned that an organism lives in an environment made of living and nonliving things. [2]But there are different kinds of environments. [3]Compare a desert and a tropical rain forest and think about how they are different. [4]Organisms survive in each of these environments. [5]Therefore, each environment meets the needs of the organisms that live in it. [6]Plants and animals in both environments are provided with shelter, food, air, and water.

B [7]When studying environments, scientists think about all the living and nonliving things in them. [8]They also study how organisms *interact* in their environment. [9]An **ecosystem** is all the living and nonliving things that interact in an environment and how they affect each other. [10]The desert, tropical rain forest, grassland, and tundra are examples of different ecosystems.

C [11]Many kinds of organisms live in different ecosystems. [12]Why can't a frog live in the desert? [13]Because it needs lots of water and insects to eat to stay alive. [14]A rain forest, though, is a perfect environment for a frog— do you know why?

D [15]A **community** is made of all living things in an ecosystem. [16]Can you name some members of a rain forest community?

E [17]A **population** is all of one kind of organism in an ecosystem, for example, all the deer in a forest. [18]A tropical rain forest has many populations. [19]Can you name a few?

F [20]The table below organizes information so you can compare ecosystems. [21]For example, it shows that a desert and the tundra support different kinds of animals.

ECOSYSTEMS				
	Desert	Rain Forest	Grass-land	Tundra
Temperature	very hot	hot	warm	very cold
Rainfall	very little	daily	often	very little
Examples of Plants	cactus, bushes	palm trees, ferns, vines	grasses, food crops	mosses, grasses
Examples of Animals	lizards, snakes, mice	birds, monkeys, insects	gophers, sheep, rabbits	polar bears, oxen, caribou

G [22]Comparing information is a useful skill. [23]Think about shopping for a bike. [24]Diagrams like the one below can help you compare and contrast skillfully.

COMPARING BICYCLES

Reason for comparing:
To find the best bike to buy

What is being compared:

Mountain bike (MB) vs. BMX racing bike

How same?	How different?
Both... • have wheels, frame, and brakes. • can be used for transportation. • operate the same. • steer the same.	• MB is big, BMX is small. • MB has multiple gears, BMX does not. • MB is used for transportation, BMX is used for racing. • MB usually costs more than BMX.

Conclusion: Unless you are going to ride long distances, a BMX is probably the best buy.

1. For each statement, circle T or F for true or false. In each blank, write the number of the <u>SENTENCE</u> that gives the best evidence for your answer.

   a. Frogs, lily pads, and fish are parts of a pond community.

   T F ____

   b. An ecosystem includes only living things.　　T F ____

   c. All the barn owls in a state park make up a population of owls.　　T F ____

   d. Squirrels and mice are two different populations of animals.　　T F ____

   e. A desert community is made up of cactus, sand, and camels.

   T F ____

   f. A desert ecosystem can include cactus, sand, and camels.　　T F ____

2. What is the most likely meaning of *interact* as it is used in sentence 8?

   a. affect each other
   b. grow together
   c. reproduce
   d. breathe

   Write the number of the other sentence (not sentence 8) that gives the best evidence for your answer. ____

3. Name an ecosystem.

   _____

   List 5 populations of organisms you would expect to find in it.

   _____

   _____

   _____

   _____

   _____

4. A **taiga** is an ecosystem that is cold in the winter, cool in the summer, has little rainfall, and supports evergreen trees, moose, and weasels. Which other ecosystem does it most resemble?

   _____

5. Complete the diagram below to compare the populations in the desert and the rain forest ecosystems.

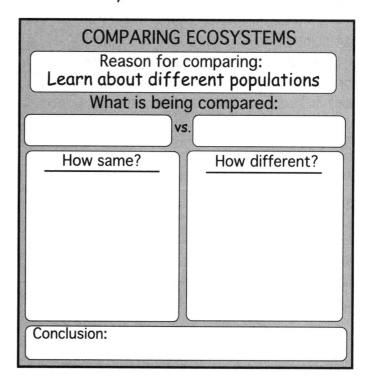

COMPARING ECOSYSTEMS
Reason for comparing:
Learn about different populations
What is being compared:

[　　　　　] vs. [　　　　　]

How same? | How different?

Conclusion:

17—Instincts, Behavior, and Survival

A [1]Organisms can live only in environments that have what they need. [2]Different environments meet the needs of different organisms. [3]For example, some animals and plants that easily live in a rain forest do not survive in a desert.

B [4]Organisms must be *equipped* with things that help them survive in an ecosystem. [5]If it is cold, they need fur to stay warm. [6]If they have enemies, they need strong muscles to run or fight. [7]If they are easily killed, they must have the ability to reproduce quickly and in large numbers. Why do you think this is necessary? [8]Things like fur, muscles, and wings, are called **structures**—they help the organism survive.

C [9]When a bird builds a nest or a spider spins a web, it is following its instincts. [10]An **instinct** is a behavior that does not have to be learned. [11]Behaviors that are not instincts must be learned. [12]For example, lion cubs and other cats are taught to hunt. [13]Seagulls are taught to drop clams to crack them open. [14]Such **learned behaviors** are gained by experience, or by being taught.

D [15]An animal has a special set of structures, instincts, and learned behaviors that helps it survive. [16]But remember, the environment within each ecosystem is unique.* [17]To predict whether or not an organism can survive in an ecosystem, you need to know about the organism's set of structures,

instincts, and learned behaviors. [18]You must also have information about the environment and the way things interact with each other within the ecosystem. [19]Knowing about the other organisms that live in an ecosystem, the temperature, and the rainfall can help you predict whether an animal can use its structures, instincts, and learned behaviors to survive there.

E [20]Below is information about animals that survive in a desert ecosystem. [21]The data table, below left, describes how many kinds of insects, snakes, cactus, birds, and rodents live there. [22]For example, there are 50 different kinds of insects. [23]The pie chart at the right is a circle that represents all the animals in the ecosystem. [24]It is easy to see that there are far more types of insects than other organisms in this desert ecosystem.

ORGANISMS FOUND IN A DESERT ECOSYSTEM

Animals	Kinds
Insects	50
Snakes	10
Cactus	15
Birds	10
Rodents	15

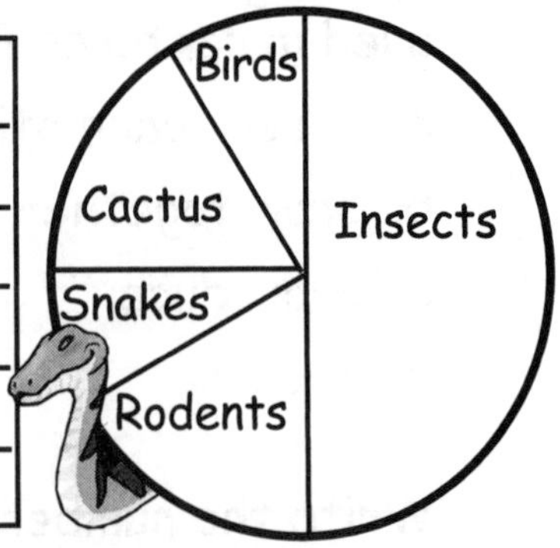

Notice that the percentages are the same as the numbers of kinds (insects are 50% of all animal kinds, etc.).

* unique: special; the only one like it

1. For each statement, circle T or F for true or false. In each blank, write the letter of the <u>PARAGRAPH</u> that gives the best evidence for your answer.

   a. Organisms survive only when their needs are met.   T F ____

   b. Ants must reproduce in large numbers to survive.   T F ____

   c. Tigers hunt by instinct.   T F ____

   d. All organisms can live in all ecosystems.   T F ____

   e. A wink of the eye is an example of learned behavior.   T F ____

2. What is the most likely meaning of *equipped* as it is used in sentence 4?

   a. taken away   c. strong
   b. provided with   d. large

3. Label each behavior below with I for Instinct or L for Learned. Write a sentence to explain each choice.

   a. A person blinks when his or her eyes get dry. ____

   _____

   _____

   _____

   b. A baby cries for a toy. ____

   _____

   _____

   _____

   c. A dog begs for a snack. ____

   _____

   _____

   _____

   d. People pull their hands away from a flame. ____

   _____

   _____

   _____

4. Use the information in the table below to complete the pie chart at the right. Label each section. (Remember, half the circle is 50%.)

   BIRDWATCHING IN THE NORTHEAST

Population	Number
Robin	50
Sparrow	25
Finch	25

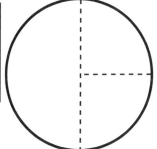

5. Complete the pie chart to match the table below. Use the first letter of each animal type to label the pie sections (I = Insects, etc.)

   ANIMALS IN THE RAIN FOREST

Animals	Kinds
Insects	600
Snakes	50
Monkeys	50
Birds	200
Frogs	100

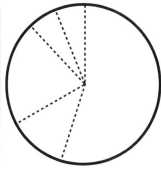

18—Plant and Animal Cells

A ¹Remember that the atom is the basic building block of matter. ²The **cell** is the building block of all living things. ³Therefore, all organisms are made up of one or more cells. ⁴The simplest organisms, such as **bacteria**, are made of one cell. ⁵Animals and plants have more than one cell. ⁶Humans are made up of trillions of cells. (⁷A trillion is a million million.)

B ⁸A **tissue** is a group of cells that all do the same thing. ⁹For example, muscle is a tissue. ¹⁰Muscle cells all *contract*, or pull together, when they move body parts. ¹¹Brain cells are also a tissue. ¹²They work together to send information. ¹³Can you name other tissues?

C ¹⁴A cell is made of many different cell parts, or **structures**. ¹⁵Each cell structure has a function. ¹⁶A **function** is the job done by a structure. ¹⁷The structures of animal cells are different from those of plant cells.

D ¹⁸All animal cells have a structure called a **cell membrane**. ¹⁹The function of the cell membrane is to separate the structures inside the cell from everything outside the cell. ²⁰Inside the animal cell is a clear jelly-like liquid called the **cytoplasm**. ²¹Floating in the cytoplasm are a number of different structures. ²²The cell needs each structure in order to survive. ²³For example, **mitochondria** are needed to provide energy for the cell. ²⁴The **nucleus** organizes the cell's activities. ²⁵Look at the diagram of an animal cell, and find the structures you read about.

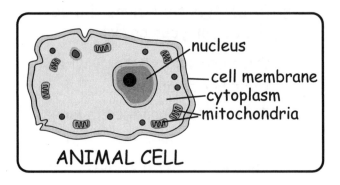

ANIMAL CELL

nucleus
cell membrane
cytoplasm
mitochondria

E ²⁶Plant cells are similar to animal cells, but they have a few different structures. ²⁷For example, plants need energy from sunlight to survive, so plant cells have a structure that changes sunlight into energy. ²⁸This structure is called a **choroplast**, and it is green. ²⁹Like animal cells, plants have a cell membrane, but they also have a *rigid* **cell wall**. ³⁰The cell wall is outside the cell membrane. ³¹Cell walls are needed to support plants because they don't have a skeleton. ³²Plants also need to store large amounts of water. ³³In plant cells, a **vacuole** is a storage sack for water and other things.

F ³⁴Look at the diagram of a typical plant cell below. ³⁵Locate the cell wall, chloroplasts, and vacuole. ³⁶Then see if you can find the nucleus, cell membrane, cytoplasm, and mitochondria.

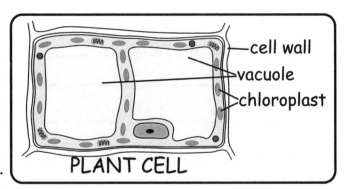

PLANT CELL

cell wall
vacuole
chloroplast

1. For each statement, circle T or F
    for true or false. In the blanks,
    write the number(s) of the
    <u>SENTENCE(s)</u> that gives the best
    evidence for your answer.

    a. All cells have the same
        structures.   T F ___

    b. All cell structures have
        jobs.   T F ___, ___

    c. Cells get energy from
        mitochondria.   T F ___

    d. A tissue is made up of cells
        that do the same thing.
                                 T F ___

2. What is the most likely meaning of
    rigid as it is used in sentence 29?
    a. stiff
    b. soft
    c. light
    d. weak

3. What structures do plant and
    animal cells have in common?

    _____

    _____

4. Heart cells make up heart tissue.
        T   F

    Write the letter of the paragraph
    that gives the best evidence for
    your answer. ___

5. What words mean the same as
    contract in sentence 10?
    a. get weaker
    b. get bigger
    c. tighten
    d. stretch

6. In the box below, draw a plant cell.
    Label the nucleus, cell membrane,
    cytoplasm, mitochondria, cell wall,
    vacuole, and chloroplast.

    ┌────────────────────────────┐
    │   │
    │   │
    │   │
    │   │
    │   │
    │   │
    └────────────────────────────┘

7. Why do you think human cells do
    not have cell walls? Use a complete
    sentence to explain.

    _____

    _____

    _____

8. Why are plants green? Use a
    complete sentence to explain.

    _____

    _____

    _____

    Write the number of the sentence
    that best supports your answer.

    ___

19—Plant Structure, Function, and Survival

A [1]To survive, a plant needs water and energy. [2]A plant also needs **minerals** from the soil and a gas called **carbon dioxide**, or **CO_2**, from the air. [3]Minerals are elements such as nitrogen and phosphorus that are found in the ground and that plants need to stay healthy. [4]Carbon dioxide is a gas that plants use to make food.

B [5]You already know that each plant cell has structures that help the cell survive. [6]The whole plant also needs structures. [7]For example, a plant has one structure to get water and a different structure to gather sunlight. [8]Plants use **roots** to get water and minerals from the soil. [9]Roots are structures that also *anchor* plants to the ground. [10]Plants trap energy from sunlight in their **leaves**. [11]Leaves also bring CO_2 gas into the plants. [12]Do you know what structures raise plants above the ground? [13]For flowers and trees, it is the **stems** and **trunks** that *elevate* the plants.

PLANT STRUCTURES

Leaves
Stem
Trunk
Roots

C [14]Sometimes it is not easy to understand what each plant structure does. [15]But often, its function can be discovered by imagining what would happen to the whole plant if one of its parts were damaged or removed.

D [16]For example, think about a bicycle. [17]What is the function of a bicycle's handlebars? [18]Answer by thinking what would happen if the handlebars were broken or missing. [19]You could not steer the bicycle. [20]Therefore, the function of handlebars is to steer a bicycle. [21]What would happen if a tire went flat? [22]The bicycle would no longer ride smoothly. [23]We can use a table to organize such information.

> Imagining what happens when a part is not working is an excellent way of finding the function of one part of a whole object.

E [24]The table below lists some bicycle parts. [25]Their functions were found by asking, "What would happen to the bicycle if the part were damaged or missing?"

PARTS OF A BICYCLE		
	If the part were missing, the bicycle would...	The function of the part is to help...
Kick-stand	fall over.	hold the bicycle up.
Brakes	be difficult to stop.	slow or stop the bicycle.
Handle-bars	not turn easily.	steer the bicycle.
Pedal	not move.	apply force to the wheels.

1. For each statement, circle T or F for true or false. In the blanks, write the number(s) of the <u>SENTENCE</u>(s) that gives the best evidence for your answer.

   a. CO_2 exists in the atmosphere as part of the air.   T F ____

   b. Phosphorus is a gas that plants need to survive.
      T F ____, ____

   c. Carbon dioxide is a mineral.
      T F ____

   d. The only function of roots is to anchor a plant.   T F ____, ____

2. What is the most likely meaning of *anchor* as used in sentence 9?

   a. loosen up

   b. hold down

   c. release from

   d. hang on

3. What would happen to a plant if some of its structures failed to function?

   _____

   _____

   _____

   Write the number of the sentence that gives the best evidence for your answer. ____

4. What is the likely meaning of *elevate* as it is used in sentence 13?

   a. bring down

   b. move sideways

   c. trim shorter

   d. make higher

5. What would be a good reason to elevate a plant?

   _____

   _____

   _____

   Write the number of the paragraph that gives the best evidence for your answer. ____

6. Think about the *Parts of a Bicycle* chart in the lesson. The function of each part was learned after thinking about what would happen if the part were missing. Use the same kind of thinking to complete the *Parts of a Plant* chart below. Also, use information about plant parts from the lesson.

PARTS OF A PLANT		
Part	If the part were missing, the plant would…	The function of the part is to help…
Leaf		
Trunk		
Stem		
Root		

20—Animals, Plants, and Energy

A [1]Animal and plant cells do work to survive, and to do work they need energy. [2]Therefore, animals and plants must get energy to survive.

B [3]Animals and plants get energy differently. [4]Animals get their energy from the food they eat. [5]As food is **digested**, it is broken down into smaller pieces. [6]These tiny food particles reach the animal's cells. [7]Inside each cell, energy is released from the particles. [8]This proces of releasing energy from food is called **respiration**. [9]During respiration, an animal uses oxygen gas and makes carbon dioxide. [10]The energy is used to do work such as hunting and reproducing. [11]Any energy the animal does not use right away is stored as fat. [12]The flow chart shows the path of energy from food to work.

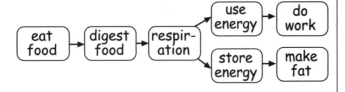

C [13]Instead of digesting food, plants get their energy right from the sun. [14]Sunlight travels across space to a plant's green leaves. [15]**Chlorophyll** in leaves *traps* the sunlight's energy. [16]The energy is used to do work such as growing, moving, and making starch. [17]Plants store energy in starch. [18]In plants, **photosynthesis** is the process that changes the energy of sunlight to energy the plants can use to do work. [19]During photosynthesis, plants use carbon dioxide and make oxygen—just the opposite of what animals do.

D [20]Animals eat plants and use plant starch as food for energy. [21]Therefore, animals need plants in order to survive. [22]The diagram below shows how a plant gets and uses energy. [23]When such events happen over and over in the same order, they *repeat*. [24]A **cycle** is a sequence of events that repeats over and over.

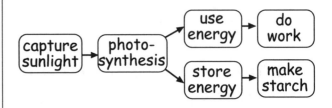

E [25]To show the sequence of steps in a cycle, a cycle diagram can be used. [26]Consider the *Day-Night Cycle* diagram. [27]Why do the arrows go in different directions?

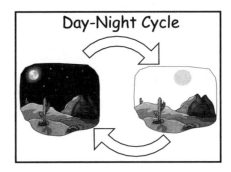

Day-Night Cycle

F [28]Now think about the *Carbon-Oxygen Cycle* below (and reread sentences 9 and 19). [29]See if you can explain how the cycle works.

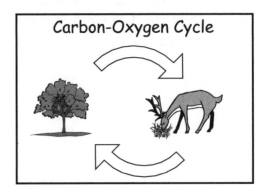

Carbon-Oxygen Cycle

1. For each statement, circle T or F for true or false. In each blank, write the number of the SENTENCE that gives the best evidence for your answer.

   a. Animals get energy from plant starch.   T F ____

   b. Plants digest food to get energy.   T F ____

   c. Animals get energy directly from the sun.   T F ____

   d. During photosynthesis, light energy is used to do work.   T F ____

2. What is the most likely meaning of *traps* as it is used in sentence 13?

   a. lets go of

   b. decreases

   c. catches

   d. blocks

3. Based on paragraphs B and C, do you think plants need animals to survive?

   Yes   No

   Write the number of the sentence that gives the best evidence for your answer. ____

4. Write each term below in its proper place in the flow chart to show the correct order for energy flow: *plant, animal, starch, sun*

5. Finish drawing a cycle diagram of the four seasons below. Draw the other three arrows, and label the boxes with the proper seasons.

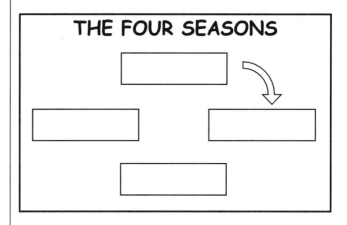

6. In the water cycle, water evaporates from the ocean and forms clouds, which cause rain that returns to the ocean. Below, use boxes and arrows to draw a diagram of the four steps of the water cycle.
   Include these words: *rain, ocean, evaporation, cloud.*

   ┌─────────────────────────────┐
   │   THE WATER CYCLE   │
   │   │
   │   │
   │   │
   │   │
   │   │
   └─────────────────────────────┘

21—Animal Needs and Animal Behavior

A [1]Animals use energy to do work. [2]For example, a lion uses energy to hunt, get shelter, and communicate. [3]Like other mammals, a lion also uses energy to keep a constant body temperature, digest food, keep its heart beating, and breathe.

B [4]In order to survive, animals must use energy to get what they need from their environment. [5]For example, if a lion is hungry, it must *track* its prey and then run fast to catch it. [6]If there is a storm, a lion must use energy to find shelter. [7]An animal uses energy to move so it can get what it needs.

C [8]When an organism reacts to something, it **responds**. [9]For example, a lion responds to thirst by drinking. [10]How would you respond to a cold day? [11]Would you add more clothing or take it off?

D [12]Anything that makes you use energy is called a **stimulus.** [13]Rain is a stimulus. [14]It makes you go inside. [15]Thirst is a stimulus. [16]It makes you get a drink. [17]Moving inside and drinking are **responses**. [18]Each of these stimuli causes a response. [19]Ducking a snowball, laughing at a joke, and coming in out of the cold are responses. [20]Responses use up energy. [21]Animals need energy to respond to stimuli in their environment. [22]Therefore, animals need energy to survive.

E [23]The response of an animal to a stimulus is called a **behavior**. [24]For example, animals respond to thirst by drinking water. [25]Drinking is a behavior.

[26]Animals respond to fear by running away. [27]Running away is a behavior, too. [28]What behavior do people show when they are happy? [29]When they are sad?

F [30]Some behaviors are responses to stimuli in the environment. [31]A typical response to cold weather is to look for shelter. [32]Other behaviors are responses to stimuli that happen inside the animal. [33]For example, thirst is an inside stimulus. [34]Can you think of another example of an inside stimulus?

G [35]Some responses are automatic. [36]When you feel cold, you shiver. [37]What happens when you touch something very hot? [38]You jerk your fingers back without thinking about it. [39]When a behavior is automatic, it is called a **reflex**. [40]When a dog scratches an itch, the scratching is a reflex.

H [41]Look at the *Animal Behavior* chart below. [42]It contains a list of stimulus/response pairs.

ANIMAL BEHAVIORS

Stimulus	Internal	External	Response
Hunger	X		Get food, eat
Flood		X	Find high ground
Getting tired	X		Sleep
Thirst	X		Find water, drink
Forest fire		X	Run away

I [43]What do you think is meant by the words *Internal* and *External* as they are used on the chart above?

1. For each statement, circle T or F for true or false. In each blank, write the number of the SENTENCE that gives the best evidence for your answer.

   a. To keep a constant body temperature, humans need food.   T F ____

   b. A stimulus causes a response.   T F ____

   c. Doing homework is a reflex.   T F ____

   d. A stimulus can come only from outside an organism.

      T F ____

2. What is the most likely meaning of *track* as it is used in sentence 5?

   a. footprint   c. follow

   b. stay away from   d. eat

3. *Internal* and *External*, used in sentence 43, probably mean stimuli that are _____ the animal.

   a. automatic and reflexive

   b. above and below

   c. inside and outside

   d. hot and cold

4. Explain how an animal responds to a forest fire. Write a complete sentence.

   _____

   _____

   _____

5. Are the following statements examples of reflexes? Circle the correct answer.

   a. A doctor hits your knee with a rubber hammer and your leg jerks up.   Yes   No

   b. Dark clouds roll in, and it begins to thunder. You run inside your house.   Yes   No

   c. You accidentally touch a hot stove. Your hand jerks away.

      Yes   No

   d. You put on the brakes of your bicycle to slow down.   Yes   No

6. Complete the chart below. Put an X in the correct column to show whether each stimulus is internal or external. State the correct response to each stimulus.

SCHOOL BEHAVIOR

Stimulus	Internal	External	Response
Hunger			
Fire alarm			
Home-work			
Thirst			
Test			

22—The Five Senses and Survival

A [1]The environment has many dangers. [2]To survive, animals need information about the world around them. [3]Imagine not having information about the weather, the time of day, or where your next meal is coming from!

B [4]How do animals get information about a *hostile* environment? [5]How do they sense danger? [6]How does a deer know that a wolf is nearby? [7]By using its eyes, ears, and nose, a deer can sense the presence of a wolf. [8]Seeing, hearing, and smelling are three **senses**. [9]Taste and touch are also senses. [10]For each sense there is a sense organ. [11]What organ is used to taste? [12]To touch?

C [13]Sense organs are connected to the brain by nerves. [14]A **nerve** carries information from sense organs to the brain. [15]A nerve is made of long cells. [16]Nerves connect the eyes, ears, nose, and other sense organs, including the skin, to the brain. [17]Information sent to the brain by nerves is *evaluated* by brain cells. [18]This information acts like a stimulus. [19]It can cause an animal to use energy to survive.

D [20]For example, if information warns of danger, the brain will cause the animal to escape.

E [21]Think of a forest fire. [22]What kinds of information would warn

animals of the danger? [23]Look at the flow chart below.

F [24]Sight and smell would warn of a forest fire, but so would other senses. [25]Think how you would show each of these senses in a flow chart.

G [26]What an animal sees, hears, smells, tastes, and touches determines what it does to survive. [27]But each sense is not the same in every animal. [28]For example, a dog's sense of smell is one hundred times better than a human's.

H [29]Not all animals have five senses. [30]For example, an earthworm gets along on only one sense organ. [31]Earthworms have skin that responds to touch.

I [32]What happens to an animal's chance of survival if its sense organs are not working properly? [33]Look at the chart below. [34]It lists problems with the major sense organs. [35]Why would it be hard to survive when sense organs are not working?

Sense Organ	Problem	Effect
Ears	Punctured ear drum	Deafness
Eyes	Cataracts	Blindness
Nose	Stuffed up nose	Can't smell
Fingertips	Burned skin	Numbness
Tastebuds	Damaged nerve	Can't taste

Sense Organ	Problem with Organ	Effect on the Animal
Ear	infection	harder to _____
Lungs	asthma	harder to _____
Brain	stroke	harder to _____
Muscles	sprain	harder to _____
Bone	broken	harder to _____

1. For each statement, circle T or F for true or false. In the blanks, write the number(s) of the <u>SENTENCE</u>(s) that gives the best evidence for your answer.

   a. Nerves connect your brain to your fingertips.   T F ____, ____

   b. Animals can survive without information.   T F ____

   c. Dogs can smell things that humans cannot.   T F ____

   d. Animals need five sense organs for survival.   T F ____

2. What is the most likely meaning of *hostile* as it is used in sentence 4?

   a. peaceful
   b. happy
   c. dangerous
   d. large

3. What senses can warn you that a busy street is dangerous?

   _____

   _____

4. What is the most likely meaning of *evaluated* as it is used in sentence 17?

   a. judged
   b. ignored
   c. changed
   d. blocked

5. The following table lists animal organs and problems that can damage them. Complete each *Effect* column.

6. The environment is filled with danger. Name the senses that would warn an animal of each danger listed below.

   a. fire _____
   b. skunk _____
   c. rattlesnake _____
   d. flood _____
   e. grizzly bear _____
   f. sour milk _____

7. A tornado is coming! Complete the flow chart to show how you would react.

   stimulus:
   [tornado]
   sense organs:
   [   ]
   information carrier:
   [   ]
   evaluation center:
   [   ]
   response:
   [   ]

23—The Life Cycle of Plants

A [1]You know that a *cycle* is a sequence of events that repeat in the same order. [2]All living things pass through life cycles. [3]For many organisms, the **stages**, or steps, of the **life cycle** include birth, growth, reproduction, and death. [4]In this lesson, we explore the life cycles of several plants.

B [5]Look at the diagram of the life cycle of a typical flowering plant below. [6]You probably know what a flower and a seed look like. [7]The first step in the life cycle is when a seed begins to grow. [8]This is called **germination**. [9]When the seed grows into a young plant, it is called a **seedling**. [10]When the seedling is *mature* enough to reproduce, it is called an **adult plant**. [11]The next step in the life cycle of a flowering plant is when an adult plant produces flowers. [12]Inside the flower are small grains called **pollen**. [13]**Pollination** happens when pollen is carried to the flower of another plant by birds and insects. [14]Pollination makes it possible for the seeds to grow. [15]Once the seeds start growing, the life cycle starts all over again.

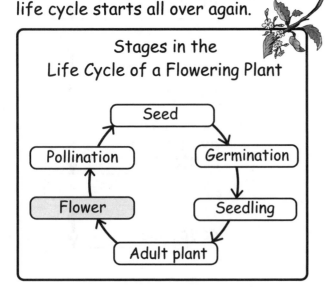

Stages in the
Life Cycle of a Flowering Plant

C [16]Not all plants produce flowers. [17]For example, the pine tree produces its seeds inside *cones*. [18]Therefore, its life cycle is a little different from the life cycle of a flowering plant. [19]Plants that produce cones are called **conifers**. [20]Hemlock and spruce are two other conifer trees. [21]Compare the life cycle of a conifer, below, to the life cycle of a flowering plant. [22]How is it different?

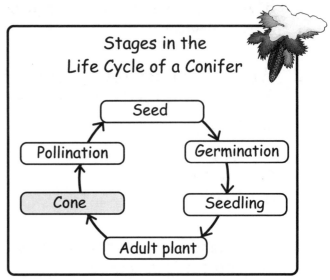

Stages in the
Life Cycle of a Conifer

D [23]There are many differences between flowers and conifers. [24]Conifers have small, narrow leaves called needles, but flowering plants have broad leaves. [25]Conifers stay green all year long. [26]Flowering plants lose their leaves in the fall. [27]Pollination in flowers is carried out by birds, bees, and other insects. [28]Pollination in conifers is carried out by the wind. [29]Lumber for building houses comes from conifers, but perfume comes from flowering plants. [30]Many flowering plants live only one year. [31]Conifers live many years.

1. For each statement, circle T or F for true or false. In the blanks, write the number(s) of the <u>SENTENCE</u>(s) that gives the best evidence for your answer.

   a. The stages in a cycle can be put in a different order.

      T F ____

   b. Pollination creates new plants.

      T F ____

   c. A plant must be a seedling before it is an adult.   T F ____

   d. A hemlock produces cones.

      T F ____, ____

2. What is the most likely meaning of *mature*, used in sentence 10?

   a. young

   b. grown up

   c. born

   d. in childhood

3. Which tree would you expect to find in a forest owned by a company that makes lumber for building houses?

   a. apple

   b. peach

   c. pine

   d. maple

   Write the letters of the paragraphs that give the best evidence for your answer. ____,

   ____

4. Wind pollinates conifers. Bees and other animals pollinate flowers. Can you think of reasons why some birds and insects might be attracted to flowers but not to pine cones?

   _____

   _____

   _____

5. Look at the life cycle diagrams in the lesson. What do you think is the function of a flower? Use a complete sentence to explain your answer.

   _____

   _____

   _____

6. Review what you have learned by filling in the boxes to complete the comparing and contrasting diagram.

COMPARING PLANTS
What is being compared:

Flowering Plant	vs.	Conifer
How same?		How different?

Conclusion:

24—The Life Cycle of Animals

A [1]All organisms go through life cycles. [2]Plants grow from seeds to seedlings into adult plants that produce flowers or cones. [3]After a flower or a cone is pollinated, new seeds grow into seedlings and the cycle continues.

B [4]Animals also pass through life cycles. [5]They are born, grow, become young animals, grow some more, and become adults. [6]Adult animals can then reproduce and have *offspring*. [7]The life cycle begins again as offspring grow into young animals.

C [8]An animal develops from a *fertilized* egg. [9]In a process called **fertilization**, male and female sex cells are combined. [10]Without fertilization, an egg will not develop into an animal.

D [11]Look at the life cycle of a typical animal below. [12]How is it different from a plant life cycle? [13]What do you think the term *adolescence* means?

E [14]Why do you think that death is not usually included in a life cycle diagram? [15]Cycles do not have a beginning or end. [16]Life passes from one organism to the next in a continuous cycle. [17]Because death is an ending, it is not included as part of a life cycle.

F [18]Death is part of the life history of one organism. [19]For example, an animal develops from a fertilized egg to birth then to infancy then to childhood then to adolescence then to old age, and then it dies. [20]What kind of diagram could be used to show the life history of an animal? [21]A flow chart is often used to show the steps in such a process—it has a beginning and an end.

G [22]Look at the flow chart. [23]It shows the stages of development in a human from birth to death. [24]Would it be possible to rearrange any of these stages? [25]Would it be possible to skip any of these stages? [26]Could this flow chart begin at any stage other than *Birth*? [27]No, nor could it end at any stage other than *Death*.

Life History of a Human

Birth
↓
Infancy
↓
Childhood
↓
Adolescence
↓
Adulthood
↓
Old age
↓
Death

H [28]Could the items in a life history be ordered differently? [29]Does the life history flow chart have a beginning and end? [30]Does the life cycle diagram have a beginning and an end?

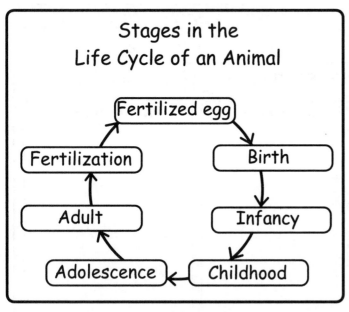

Stages in the Life Cycle of an Animal

Fertilized egg

Fertilization

Birth

Adult

Infancy

Adolescence

Childhood

1. For each statement, circle T or F for true or false. In the blanks, write the letter(s) of the <u>PARAGRAPH</u>(s) that gives the best evidence for your answer.

   a. A life history has a beginning and an end.   T F ____, ____

   b. A life cycle has a beginning and an end.   T F ____

   c. Fertilization creates a new animal.   T F ____

   d. Old age is the end of any life history.   T F ____, ____

2. What is the most likely meaning of *offspring* as it is used in sentence 6?

   a. parents

   b. metal spirals

   c. children

   d. grandparents

3. Why is *death* not given as a stage in the life cycle of an animal? (See the diagram in the lesson.)

   _____

   _____

   _____

   Write the number of the paragraph that gives the best evidence for your answer. ____

4. Can you change the order of items

   a. in a cycle?   Yes   No

   b. in a flow chart?   Yes   No

5. A life span can be defined as the longest period of time an organism can live. For example, the oldest humans live to be about 120 years old.

Life Spans of Animals

Animal	Life Span in Years
Fox	8
Queen ant	15
Goldfish	30
Orangutan	50
Alligator	60
Whale	80

Use the information in the *Life Spans* table above to complete the bar graph below.

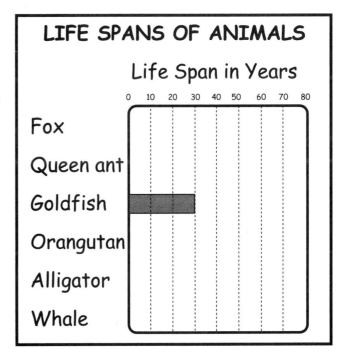

25—Heredity

A [1]Which rabbit is most likely to survive in snowy Alaska? [2]One that is white or one that is brown? [3]White, of course. [4]Where do you think the color of a rabbit's fur comes from? [5]It comes from the rabbit's parents. [6]This lesson is about the passing of characteristics like fur color from parent to offspring.

B [7]**Offspring** are the children of people or the young of animals. [8]Pups are the offspring of dogs. [9]Cubs are the offspring of bears or lions. [10]Can you think of other types of offspring?

C [11]**Characteristics** is a category used to describe how an object looks. [12]For example, fur color is a characteristic of rabbits. [13]Seed shape is a characteristic of pea plants.

D [14]However, when describing specific characteristics of organisms, scientists use a different term. [15]A **trait** is an exact characteristic of an organism. [16]For example, white fur and brown fur are traits of a rabbit. [17]Smooth or wrinkled seeds are traits of a pea plant. [18]Can you name three traits of a person you know?

E [19]Many traits come from parents. [20]The process by which traits are *transferred* from parents to offspring is called **heredity**. [21]You **inherit** a trait from your parents when you receive it from them. [22]A trait that is transferred from parent to child is called an **inherited trait**. [23]For example, if your mom and dad have brown hair and you have brown hair, then you inherited this trait from your parents.

F [24]Inherited traits give only part of the picture when we describe an organism. [25]Other traits are learned. [26]You get a **learned trait** by interacting with the environment. [27]Skills such as riding a bicycle or playing the piano are learned.

G [28]Look at the *Animal Traits* table below. [29]Try to name other inherited and learned traits for each animal.

Animal Traits		
Animal	Inherited Trait	Learned Trait
Tiger	Black stripes	Hunt
Duck	Webbed feet	Swim
Rat	Long Tail	Run maze
Horse	Hair color	Trot, jump
Parrot	Feather color	Talk
Sheep dog	Long fur	Herd sheep
Dolphin	Hold breath	Do tricks
Seal	Fur color	Balance ball

1. For each statement, circle T or F for true or false. In the blanks, write the letter(s) of the <u>PARAGRAPH</u>(s) that gives the best evidence for your answer.

   a. A brown rabbit can survive best where the surroundings are brown.   T   F ____

   b. Blue eyes are a learned trait.   T   F ____

   c. A child inherits driving skills from a parent.   T   F ____, ____

2. What is the most likely meaning of *tranferred* as it is used in sentences 20 and 22?

   a. passed

   b. damaged

   c. changed

   d. erased

3. Children usually look like their parents because of which kind of trait? Circle one.

        inherited   learned

   Use complete sentences to explain your answer.

   _____

   _____

   _____

   _____

   Write the letter of the paragraph that gives the best evidence for your answer. ____

4. Complete the chart below. Put a check mark in the correct columns to show whether each trait is inherited or learned. Use the Animal Traits table in the lesson as a guide.

Animal Traits

Animal Trait	Inherited	Learned
Size of a cat's paw	✔	
A dog's tricks		
Color of insect wing		
Shape of shark's tooth		
Hunting		

5. Complete the chart below by putting a check in the correct column for each trait.

Human Traits

Human Trait	Inherited	Learned
Eye color		
Hair color		
Reading ability		
Playing hockey		
Height		
Dancing		
Cooking		
Curly hair		

26—Food Chains and Food Webs

A [1]Every organism needs food. [2]Food provides energy, and an organism will die if it does not get enough energy. [3]Plants get energy from sunlight and use it to make their food. [4]Animals get their energy by eating plants or by eating animals that eat plants.

B [5]Because plants make their own food, they are called food **producers**. [6]Animals cannot produce food—they must *consume* plants or other animals to get food. [7]Animals are called **consumers**.

C [8]Without producers, consumers would not live long. [9]That's because animals eat plants or other animals that eat plants. [10]If plants disappeared, animals would run out of food and die.

D [11]A special type of diagram is used to show what-eats-what in an ecosystem. [12]This diagram is called a **food chain.** [13]A food chain is a kind of flow chart.

E [14]In a food chain, each organism is called a link. [15]Arrows show the direction energy flows between links. [16]Each arrow means "is eaten by." [17]For example, 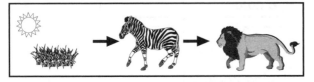 means "grass is eaten by a zebra."

F [18]Different animals may eat the same kind of consumer.

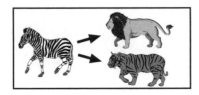

G [19]On the other hand, one kind of animal may eat more than one kind of consumer. [20]A lion eats both zebra and antelope. [21]Where would you draw two arrows to show the flow of energy in the flow chart below?

H [22]It is easier to use names instead of drawing pictures in a flow chart. [23]How would you read this flow chart?

☀ | Grass | | Zebra | | Lion |

I [24]A single food chain does not tell how all the organisms in an ecosystem relate to one another. [25]We can learn a lot about an ecosystem by putting several food chains in one diagram. [26]A diagram that combines more than one food chain is called a **food web**. [27]Think about the food web below.

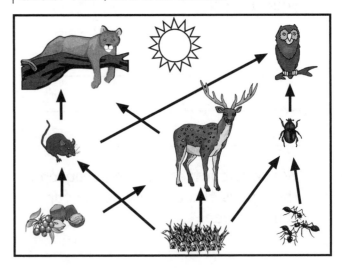

1. For each statement, circle T or F for true or false. In the blanks, write the number(s) of the <u>SENTENCE</u>(s) that gives the best evidence for your answer.

   a. An animal can be a producer.
                                 T F ____

   b. A mouse is a consumer.
                                 T F ____

   c. Producers get energy from the sun.   T F ____, ____

   d. Consumers can survive without producers.   T F ____

2. What is the most likely meaning of *consume* as it is used in sentence 6?

   a. change into   c. feed

   b. take in   d. become

3. Why is the sun part of a food chain? Use complete sentences to explain your answer.

   _____

   _____

   _____

   Write the number of the sentence that gives the best evidence for your answer. ____

4. If plants disappeared, could animals continue to survive? ____

   Use complete sentences to explain why or why not.

   _____

   _____

   _____

5. Using the food web in the lesson, complete the following food chains of the owl and the cougar.

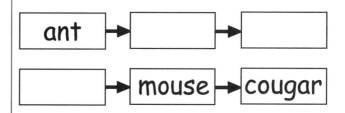

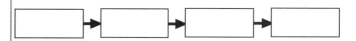

6. Write the names of the following organisms in the correct order in the flow chart below:
   fish, sea grass, shark, and shrimp.

7. Look again at the food web in the lesson. Then complete the diagram below by adding names and connecting them with arrows.

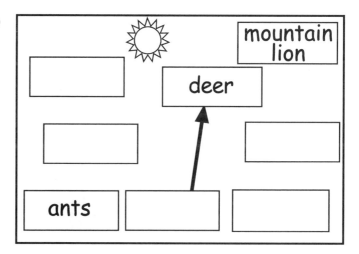

27—Organisms Change Environments

A [1]You have already learned that an *environment* is all the living and nonliving things that surround an organism. [2]An *ecosystem* is all the living and nonliving things in an environment *and* how they interact with each other.

B [3]In this lesson you will learn about how ecosystems are changed by the organisms that live in them. [4]Can you think of a way an animal or plant changes its environment? [5]Think of how beaver dams or insects that eat crops could damage the environment.

C [6]What if a disease killed all the mountain lions in the forest? [7]What do you think would happen to the number of deer? [8]The deer population would grow quickly. Why?

D [9]Deer eat shrubs that grow close to the ground. [10]What would happen to the number of shrubs if a disease wiped out all the mountain lions? [11]Many more shrubs would be eaten because there would be more deer to eat them.

E [12]Grasses and small shrubs keep soil from *eroding* during rain storms. [13]If a disease killed all the mountain lions, the deer would increase, the plants could disappear, and the forest floor could erode. [14]When the forest floor erodes, lots of soil gets washed away and ends up in streams and rivers. [15]If too much soil gets into streams and rivers, many fish will die.

F [16]The example of the mountain lion shows that organisms can change their environment. [17]Notice how easily an ecosystem can be damaged by what happens to one kind of organism. [18]In the example, a disease that killed one kind of organism led to a change in the numbers of plants and other animals. [19]What else changed?

G [20]We can record the sequence of events from the example in a flow chart. [21]The flow chart shown at the right shows the process by which a mountain lion can change its environment. [22]It shows that one change in an ecosystem can lead to another. [23]Can you think of more changes that could be added to this chart? [24]What might happen if the number of fish suddenly *plummeted* as a result of soil erosion?

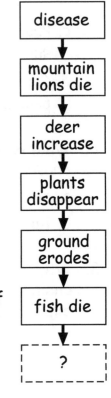

disease

↓

mountain lions die

↓

deer increase

↓

plants disappear

↓

ground erodes

↓

fish die

↓

?

H [25]There are other examples of how organisms change their environments. [26]Flies, ticks, and mosquitoes spread malaria, sleeping sickness, yellow fever, and Lyme disease. [27]Insects such as termites destroy trees. [28]However, organisms can also change the environment in a good way. [29]For example, birds often eat insects that are harmful, and grass prevents soil erosion.

1. For each statement, circle T or F for true or false. In each blank, write the letter of the <u>PARAGRAPH</u> that gives the best evidence for your answer.

   a. If the number of mountain lions grows, there will soon be more deer.　　　　T　F ___

   b. Plants cannot change the environment.　　　　T　F ___

   c. Mountain lions can keep fish from dying.　　　　T　F ___

   d. Killing certain insects can stop the spread of disease.

   　　　　　　　　　T　F ___

2. What is the most likely meaning of *plummeted* as it is used in sentence 24?

   a. doubled

   b. went up suddenly

   c. went down suddenly

   d. stayed the same

3. Plants are eaten by a mouse, which is eaten by a hawk. But hawks also eat chickens.

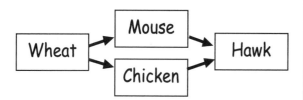

   Complete the following flow chart to show what might happen to a wheat field if farmers kill the hawks to protect the chickens.

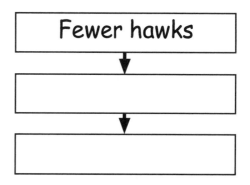

4. What would happen to the fish if more and more plants grew in the shallow pond below? Explain your answer using a complete sentence.

   _____

   _____

   _____

5. As the pond gets older, the number of plants increases. When they die, they fall to the bottom of the pond, rot, and become mud. After a very long time, what do you think will happen to the pond? Use a complete sentence to explain your answer.

   _____

   _____

   _____

28—People Change Environments

A [1]You have learned that organisms can produce good and bad changes in their environment. [2]Most changes made by organisms are small and occur over very long periods of time.

B [3]On the other hand, people can cause big changes in a short period of time. Why? [4]People use machines, which cause *immense* changes in the environment.

C [5]Consider a river flowing through a desert ecosystem. [6]What changes would be caused by building a dam across the river? [7]A lake would be formed behind the dam, and many organisms would drown. [8]Water would become available for irrigation. [9]Therefore, some of the desert would be changed into farmland.

D [10]Think about how a forest is changed when a farm is created in it. [11]What are some of these changes?

E [12]People have learned to change their environment to survive and to make it more comfortable to live in. [13]For example, trees are cut down to get wood for building houses. [14]Wide roads are cut through a forest to speed up the flow of traffic. [15]Coal used for heating is dug out of the ground, which creates huge holes. [16]Most of these changes *harm* the environment.

F [17]People produce many kinds of poisonous chemicals when they make things in factories. [18]These chemicals can kill animals and plants. [19]Harmful materials like these chemicals are called **pollutants**. [20]Adding these pollutants to the environment results in **pollution**. [21]There are many kinds of pollutants. [22]For example, car exhaust, is a pollutant that causes **air pollution**. [23]Oil spilled in the ocean is a pollutant, and it causes **water pollution**.

G [24]A pie chart is a circle diagram that shows the parts that make up a whole. [25]The pie chart below shows how different sources of pollution can pollute one city. (Note: [26]One ton is equal to 2000 pounds. [27]A small car weighs about one ton.)

H [28]Many of the changes made to the environment by people kill living organisms. [29]These living things may disappear completely and are called *endangered species*. [30]People are trying to protect the environment from damage and save endangered species. [31]Can you think of ways to help?

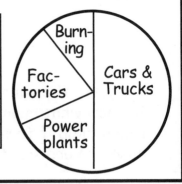

SOURCES OF AIR POLLUTION

Sources of Pollutant	Tons
Cars & Trucks	50
Factories	20
Power plants	20
Burning	10

1. For each statement, circle T or F for true or false. In each blank, write the number of the <u>PARAGRAPH</u> that gives the best evidence for your answer.

   a. Only people can change the environment.   T   F ____

   b. Building an airport can harm the environment.   T   F ____

   c. Changing the environment can help people survive.   T   F ____

2. What is the most likely meaning of *immense* as it is used in sentence 4?

   a. strange   c. small
   b. usual   d. large

3. When settlers came to America, they cut down many forests. How did this change the environment? Explain your answer using complete sentences.

   _____

   _____

   _____

4. How does the creation of a national park, like Yellowstone, help the environment? Use complete sentences to explain your answer.

   _____

   _____

   _____

5. In one area, the endangered species include 5 kinds of fish, 10 reptiles, 15 birds, 20 mammals, and 55 plants.

   Use this information to complete the table and pie graph below.

Endangered Species

Organisms	Number
Fish	
Reptiles	
Birds	
Mammals	
Plants	

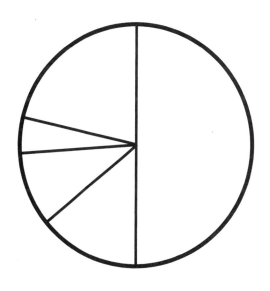

Unit III
EARTH SCIENCE

29—Earth Science and Earth Materials

A [1]**Earth Science** is the study of the things in and around the earth, such as rocks, minerals, oceans, the atmosphere, and objects in the sky. [2]The study of weather is called **meteorology**. [3]A **meteorologist** is a scientist who studies the weather. [4]The study of rocks is **geology**, and a **geologist** studies rocks and minerals. [5]The study of oceans is **oceanography**, and a scientist who studies oceans is an **oceanographer.** [6]**Astronomy** is the study of planets, moons, stars, and other objects in the sky. [7]Can you guess what we call a scientist who studies these things?

B [8]This lesson will focus on the materials that make up the earth. [9]Earth scientists study and describe the earth and its atmosphere. [10]The earth is made up of rocks, minerals, soil, water, and gases.

C [11]The materials that make up the earth change over time. [12]These changes are caused by forces. [13]Do you know what changes are produced by the force of large waves on the beach? [14]The shape of the beach changes as beach sand is pushed around by waves. [15]What force moves sand around in the desert? [16]The force of the wind pushes sand around and creates sand dunes. [17]Do you know what force created the Grand Canyon? [18]It was the force of running water.

D [19]Many of the changes to the earth's surface come from forces within the earth itself, so we must look at what the earth is made of. [20]The earth is a *sphere* that is about 8000 miles (13,000 km) in diameter. [21]The surface is solid, hard, and cool. [22]Much of the inside of the earth is liquid metal. [23]But at its center, the earth is solid and extremely hot. [24]The closer to the center of the earth, the higher the temperature. [25]The diagram below shows the name of each layer and its average temperature.

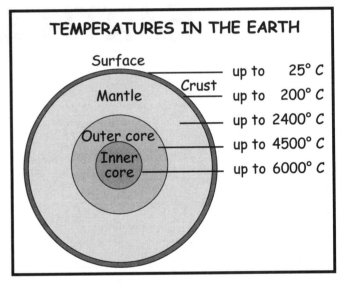

TEMPERATURES IN THE EARTH

Surface — up to 25° C
Crust — up to 200° C
Mantle — up to 2400° C
Outer core — up to 4500° C
Inner core — up to 6000° C

E [26]Look at the table, below left. [27]It contains information about the temperature of the earth. [28]Consider the graph at the right. [29]What does it tell you about the temperature as you travel deeper into the earth?

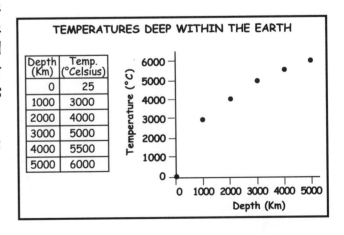

TEMPERATURES DEEP WITHIN THE EARTH

Depth (Km)	Temp. (°Celsius)
0	25
1000	3000
2000	4000
3000	5000
4000	5500
5000	6000

1. For each statement, circle T or F for true or false. In each blank, write the number of the SENTENCE that gives the best evidence for your answer.

   a. A meteorologist is a scientist who studies meteors.   T F ____

   b. Temperature increases from the center of the earth towards its surface.   T F ____

   c. The earth is completely solid.
                              T F ____

2. In sentence 20, *sphere* probably means

   a. cube.   c. ball.

   b. circle.   d. rock.

3. Which unit of length is longer, a mile or a kilometer? _____

   Write the number of the sentence that gives the best evidence for your answer. ____

4. Use the information in the lesson to complete the table below.

What is studied	Science	Scientist
rocks		
		astronomer
	meteorology	
oceans		

5. Next to each temperature, write the correct layer of the earth.

   a. 2600° _____

   b. 2000° _____

   c. 180° _____

   d. 5900° _____

   e. 20° _____

6. The temperature changes the higher you go above the earth. Use the table and graph below to answer the questions that follow.

TEMPERATURE OF THE ATMOSPHERE ABOVE EARTH

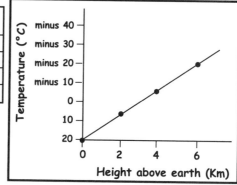

Height (Km)	Temp. (°C)
0	20
2	5
4	minus 5
6	minus 20

   a. What two things are listed in the data table? _____ and _____ .

   b. What is the distance between numbers on the horizontal (across) axis ?_____ km

   c. What happens to the temperature as you go higher above the earth?

   _____

   _____

   d. What is colder, minus 10° or minus 20°? _____

   e. At 1 km above the earth, what is the temperature? _____ km

30—Earth Materials and Their Uses

A [1]The earth is made up of a variety of materials, such as rocks, minerals, and metals. [2]People can use these resources in many ways—but first, they have to get them.

B [3]We get many earth materials by digging into the earth's crust. [4]The **earth's crust** is a thin layer of solid rock that makes up the earth's outer layer. [5]It is about 20 miles (32 km) thick.

C [6]**Rock** is made of one or more minerals stuck together. [7]**Minerals** are solid, nonliving substances found in the earth's crust. [8]A mineral is made of one or more elements. [9]For example, limestone is a mineral made up of calcium, carbon, and oxygen. [10]An **element** is a basic substance made of only one kind of matter.

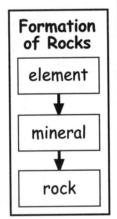

Formation of Rocks

element → mineral → rock

D [11]People use rocks to build things, such as stone walls. [12]Rocks are also used to make other building materials, such as concrete.

E [13]Minerals have many uses. [14]For example, table salt is used to make food taste better. [15]Minerals such as diamonds and gemstones are used to make jewelry. [16]Because they are so hard, diamonds are also used in drills or cutting machines. [17]Coins are often made from *pure* materials such as gold and silver. [18]Each of these metals is made of a single element. [19]Can you give

two examples of metals used to build things like bridges and automobiles?

F [20]People also use the earth as a source of energy. [21]For example, the inside of the earth is so hot that its heat can be used to boil water. [22]Boiling water makes steam. [23]Steam is a force that can be used to produce electricity. [24]The energy in hot water can also be used to heat homes. [25]Some of the earth's minerals are also used as a source of energy. [26]For example, radioactive elements like uranium are used to produce nuclear energy. [27]Fossil fuels like fuel oil and coal also come from the earth.

G [28]The water that covers most of the surface of the earth is another natural resource. [29]We use the oceans in transporting goods and people by boat. [30]If necessary, we can remove the salt to make drinking water. [31]We can even use the motion of ocean waves to produce electricity.

H [32]The circle graph below shows the major elements that make up the earth's crust. [33]About how much of the earth's crust is made up of oxygen?

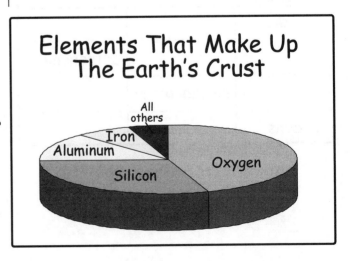

Elements That Make Up The Earth's Crust

1. For each statement, circle T or F for true or false. In each blank, write the number of the SENTENCE that gives the best evidence for your answer.

   a. Diamonds are used in drills to make them more attractive.

      T F ____

   b. An element can be broken down into compounds.   T F ____

   c. The motion of ocean waves produces a force.   T F ____

2. What is the most likely meaning of *pure* as it is used in sentence 17?

   a. unmixed   c. dirty

   b. mixed   d. valuable

3. Sodium chloride is a mineral made up of two elements, sodium and chlorine. Therefore, sodium chloride is

   a. an element.

   b. an atom.

   c. a compound.

   d. a rock.

4. The metal copper is made up of only one kind of matter. Therefore, copper is

   a. an element.

   b. an atom.

   c. a compound.

   d. a rock.

5. Use the *Elements that Make Up the Earth's Crust* pie chart in the lesson to answer the following questions.

   a. Which element is there most of in the earth's crust?

      _____

      How can you tell from the pie chart?

      _____

   b. Which element is there less of, iron or aluminum?

      _____

      Why is this difficult to answer?

      _____

      _____

   c. The earth's crust has over 90 elements. Why do you think the pie chart in the lesson shows only a few of these? Use a complete sentence to explain your answer.

      _____

      _____

      _____

6. Complete the flow chart below to show what makes up a rock, starting with its most complex part to its simplest. Use these terms:

   mineral
   compound
   rock
   element

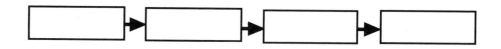

31—Minerals

A [1]If you found something that looked like gold, would it be important to find out if it was real? [2]Of course! [3]There are many kinds of minerals, and some of them appear very much alike. [4]Minerals are made up of elements and compounds that are *cemented* together. [5]These elements and compounds give the mineral certain physical properties. [6]To identify a mineral, a geologist checks four different physical properties. [7]They are luster, hardness, color, and streak.

B [8]**Luster** is a measure of the shininess of a mineral. [9]Silver and gold are examples of shiny minerals. [10]**Hardness** is a measure of how difficult it is to scratch a mineral. [11]A diamond is very hard. [12]**Color** is another way to identify a mineral. [13]The surface color of a mineral can be different from its inside color. [14]Scientists can find the inside color of a mineral by making a **streak**. [15]To make a streak, you rub the mineral against a hard surface. [16]This leaves a long mark of mineral powder showing the inner color of a mineral.

C [17]Because many minerals appear similar, it is necessary to test more than one physical property in order to correctly identify them. [18]Fool's gold looks like real gold, so checking surface color is not enough. [19]Fool's gold leaves a dark green streak. [20]But if you see a yellow streak, you're in luck!

D [21] In your house, a scale is an instrument used to measure weight.

[22]But in geology, a **scale** is a series of measurements. [23]For example, the hardness scale is a series of measurements between soft and hard. [24]Numbers from 1 to 10 represent the hardness of a mineral. [25]A soft mineral like talc has a hardness of 1 or 2 and is easily scratched. [26]A diamond has a hardness of 10. [27]Hardness of all other minerals is between 1 and 10.

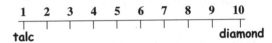

E [28]The scale for luster uses words instead of numbers. [29]In the luster scale, *metallic* is shiny like a metal, *glassy* is shiny like glass, and *dull* is not shiny at all.

F [30]Consider the table below. [31]It describes minerals using the four physical properties discussed in this lesson.

IDENTIFYING MINERALS				
Mineral	Luster	Hardness	Color (surface)	Streak
Pyrite (fool's gold)	metallic	6.5	gold-yellow	green-black
Halite (rock salt)	glassy	2.5	colorless	white
Mica	glassy	5.5	silver	silver
Talc	dull	1	white	white
Hematite (iron ore)	metallic	5	reddish-brown	reddish-brown
Galena (lead ore)	metallic	2.5	silver gray	gray
Quartz	glassy	7	white or pink	white
Hornblend	glassy	5.5	green-black	brown-gray

1. For each statement, circle T or F for true or false. In the blanks, write the number(s) of the SENTENCE(s) that give the best evidence for your answer.

   a. A mineral is made of a single element.   T F ___

   b. Real gold leaves a yellow streak.   T F ___ , ___

   c. A mineral with a hardness of 5 is softer than talc.   T F ___

2. What is the most likely meaning of *cemented*, as used in sentence 4?

   a spread
   b. joined
   c. separated
   d. made larger

Use the *Identifying Minerals* table in the lesson to answer questions 3 and 4.

3. a. Which mineral is softest?
      _____

   b. Which mineral is hardest?
      _____

   c. Which mineral gives a white streak and is dull?
      _____

   d. Which element is from a metallic reddish-brown rock?
      _____

   e. Which two properties should you check to tell the difference between halite and quartz?
      _____ , _____

4. Two mineral samples produce a grayish streak. One of the minerals is harder than the other. What is it?
   _____

5. Two minerals are rated 4 on the hardness scale. They both appear to be white. Describe how you could decide what they are. Use complete sentences.
   _____
   _____
   _____

6. The best way to understand a scale is to create one and use it. Make a scale using four different words to rate summer activities on how enjoyable they are. What words will you use?
   _____ , _____ ,
   _____ , _____

Now, use them to rate the activities below:

ACTIVITY	RATING
Biking	_____
Theme park	_____
Camping	_____
Jet skiing	_____
Summer school	_____
Travel	_____
Surfing	_____
Yardwork	_____
Pop concert	_____
Visiting museum	_____

32—Rocks and the Rock Cycle

A [1]Rocks are made up of minerals—and there are many different minerals in the earth. [2]However, rocks are not classified by the minerals that make them up. [3]Rather, they are classified by how they were formed. [4]The three types of rock are igneous, sedimentary, and metamorphic.

B [5]The *molten* layer of rock beneath the earth's crust is called **magma.** [6]Sometimes magma moves into the crust then cools and hardens into **igneous rock**. [7]Granite is an example of igneous rock.

C [8]**Sediment** is made up of small pieces of rock, minerals, and the skeletons of small animals that sink to the bottom of a river, lake, or ocean. [9]**Sedimentary rock** is formed from particles of sediment that become cemented together by pressure. [10]The pressure comes from the weight of more and more layers of sediment piling up on top of it. [11]Sandstone and limestone are examples of sedimentary rocks.

D [12]Sometimes igneous and sedimentary rocks can be changed by forces inside the earth. [13]For example, the extreme pressure and heat inside the earth can change an igneous or sedimentary rock into a **metamorphic rock**.

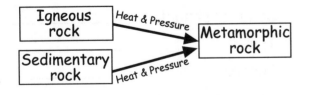

E [14]Metamorphic rock is sometimes pushed up to the earth's surface by earthquakes or the forces that make mountains. [15]Marble is an example of a metamorphic rock that was once a sedimentary rock called limestone.

E [16]Other forces can also change rocks. [17]For example, the breaking down of rocks by the force of wind and running water is called **weathering.** [18]A boulder can be worn down to a pebble by running water in a stream. [19]Rocks that are not protected from high winds will gradually wear away. [20]Water gets into cracks in rocks and then freezes and expands, causing rocks to break into smaller pieces.

F [21]A cycle diagram is used to show events that happen over and over. [22]For example, the *Rock Cycle* diagram below shows how rocks can change from one kind to another.

THE ROCK CYCLE

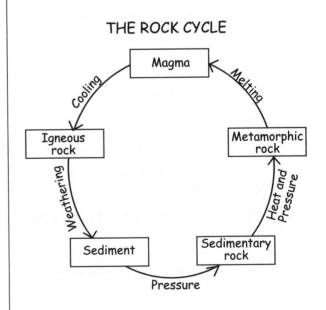

1. For each statement, circle T or F for true or false. In the blanks, write the number(s) of the SENTENCE(s) that give the best evidence for your answer.

    a. Minerals that make up granite are hardened together.
        T F ___, ___

    b. Sedimentary rock never changes.   T F ___, ___

    c. Metamorphic rock forms on the earth's surface.   T F ___, ___

2. What is the most likely meaning of *molten* as used in sentence 5?

    a. melted

    b. hardened

    c. loose

    d. solid

    Write the number of the sentence that gives the best evidence for your answer. ___

3. The bottom of a lake is covered with huge amounts of small particles. Over a long period of time this material can become what kind of rock?

    _____

    Use a complete sentence to explain how this would happen.

    _____

    _____

    _____

4. In the diagram below, some lines have been added to *The Rock Cycle* diagram from the lesson. Add arrowheads to the dotted lines and correctly label them using information from the lesson.

THE ROCK CYCLE

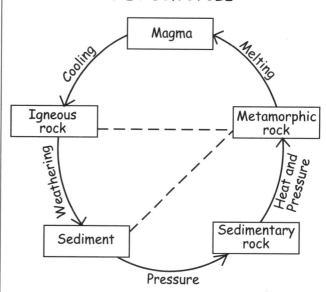

5. Explain how marble can turn back into limestone. Be sure to use complete sentences.

    _____

    _____

    _____

    _____

33—Soils

A [1]A **soil** is a mixture of rock particles, minerals, water, air, and decayed material. [2]Decayed material comes from dead animals and plants. [3]Any soil material that was once alive is called **humus**. [4]Look at the pie chart below. [5]It shows the *composition* of a typical soil.

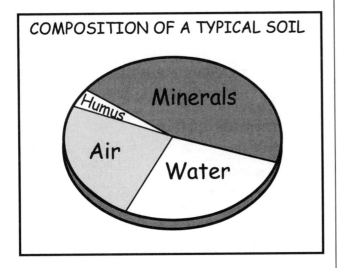

COMPOSITION OF A TYPICAL SOIL

B [6]Soils come mostly from rocks that were broken into very small pieces by the process of weathering*. [7]Rocks are made up of minerals. [8]As rocks are broken down into smaller and smaller particles, their minerals are released and become a major part of soil.

* weathering: the breakdown of rocks into smaller and smaller pieces by wind, water, and changes in temperature.

C [9]The three basic soils are sand, silt, and clay. [10]**Clay** is made up of extremely small particles that can be seen only by using a powerful microscope. [11]**Silt** is made of particles that are bigger than clay particles. [12]**Sand** particles are much larger than silt particles and are loosely packed. [13]You can feel the difference between these materials when you rub them between your fingers. [14]You can easily identify the smooth texture of clay and the rough texture of sand.

D [15]When the three basic types of soil particles are mixed together in different amounts, different textures of soil are produced. [16]For example, soil that feels sandy is made up of mostly sand. [17]However, sandy soil also contains some silt and some clay. [18]The pie graph at right shows the make-up of sandy soil. [19]Which type of particles are there the most of?

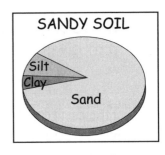

SANDY SOIL

E [20]Loam is a mixture of soil that is good for growing plants. [21]It feels less gritty than sandy soil. [22]Compare the loam and sandy soil pie charts. [23]Can you explain why loam has a smoother texture than sandy soil?

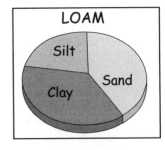

LOAM

1. For each statement, circle T or F for true or false. In the blanks, write the number(s) of the SENTENCE(s) that give the best evidence for your answer.

   a. Soils with decayed matter contain humus.   T F ___, ___

   b. Clay particles are smaller than silt particles.   T F ___

   c. Soil texture depends upon the amounts of silt, clay, and sand.   T F ___

2. What is the most likely meaning of *composition* as used in sentence 5?

   a. shape

   b. name

   c. kind

   d. makeup

3. A typical soil is made up mostly of solid material.   True   False

   Explain your answer using a complete sentence or two.

   _____

   _____

4. Could a soil sample from the moon contain humus?   Yes   No

   Explain your answer using a complete sentence or two.

   _____

   _____

   _____

5. Desert soil is nearly all sand. Deserts cover about 10% of the earth's surface. Look at the *Deserts* data table below.

DESERTS OF THE WORLD	
Location	Size (sq. miles)
North American	500,000
Australian	1,300,000
African	3,720,000
South American	260,000
Arabian	1,000,000
Asian	200,000
Indian	230,000

   In the space below, list the desert location in order from smallest to largest.

   _____

   _____

   _____

   _____

6. The soil shown in the pie graph below is about 40% clay, 35% sand, and 25% silt. Use this information to correctly label the graph.

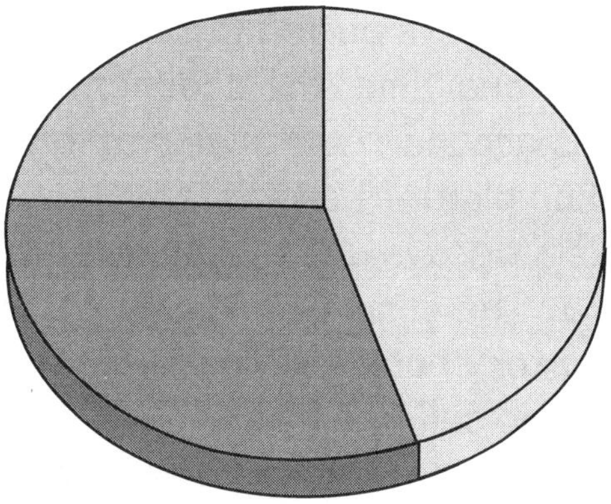

34—Fossils

A [1]**Fossils** are remains of animals that lived long ago and are often found in sedimentary rock. [2]To understand fossils, let's see how sedimentary rock is formed.

B [3]**Sediments** are small pieces of rock and other materials that settle to the bottom of oceans, lakes, and rivers. [4]Over a very long time, sediments can form rocks known as *sedimentary rocks*.

C [5]Sedimentary rocks form in layers. [6]If you sliced through the rock at the bottom of an ocean, you would see layers something like the ones in the diagram at right. [7]Such a diagram is called a **cross section**. [8]Which of the layers do you think is the oldest? [9]Which is youngest? Why? [10]If you found an object in layer 5, would it be older or younger than one found in layer 4? Why?

LAYERS OF SEDIMENTARY ROCK

D [11]When an organism dies, it sometimes gets buried in sediment. [12]Over a long time, the sediment hardens around the remains of the animal or plant. [13]Long after the organism decays and disappears, the shape of the organism remains in the sedimentary rock. [14]A fossil created this way is called a **mold**. [15]The sedimentary rock keeps a record of the shape of the organism.

E [16]Another kind of fossil is an **imprint**. [17]An imprint is made when an organism's body is pressed into sediments that later become hard.

F [18]**Paleontology** is the study of organisms that once lived on the earth. [19]**Paleontologists** search for imprints and molds of prehistoric organisms. [20]Some fossils found by paleontologists are footprints that were *preserved* in rocks. [21]Some footprint fossils tell us about the size of dinosaurs. [22]Others give us clues about how these ancient animals walked and hunted. [23]Is a footprint an imprint or a mold?

G [24]Most fossils discovered by paleontologists are imprints or molds of animals and plants that decayed very long ago. [25]However, the hard parts of an organism that have survived a very long time—like bone, shell, or seed—are also called fossils.

H [26]A fossil can also be a *preserved* organism. [27]This special fossil shows exactly what the animal looked like. [28]Animals like the wooly mammoth have been found preserved in ice. [29]Cold temperatures slow the decay of the animal's body. [30]Dry environments also slow decay. [31]The hot, dry desert sand has preserved human mummies for more than 5000 years.

I [32]Other organisms become fossils after being petrified. [33]**Petrified** means turned to stone. [34]Wood and bone are examples of materials that may be found petrified.

1. For each statement, circle T or F for true or false. In each blank, write the letter of the PARAGRAPH that gives the best evidence for your answer.

   a. Fossils are often found in igneous rock.

   T F ____

   b. A fossil of a deep footprint is a clue that the animal was heavy.

   T F ____

   c. The study of prehistoric organisms is called *geology*.

   T F ____

   d. Fossil molds can show the detailed shape of an organism.

   T F ____

2. What is the most likely meaning of *preserved* as it is used in sentences 20 and 26?

   a. broken   c. lost
   b. saved   d. destroyed

3. Preserved mummies are never found in the rain forest. Use complete sentences to explain why.

   _____

   _____

   _____

   Write the letter of the paragraph that gives the best evidence for your answer. ____

4. Similar sedimentary layers of rock can be found all over the world. The diagram below shows sedimentary rock layers in two states. Layers shown with the same patterns are the same age.

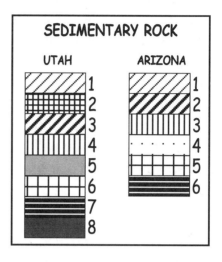

Consider the sedimentary rock layers in Utah and Arizona. Think about how they are the same and how they are different. Then answer the following questions.

a. How many sedimentary rock layers do Utah and Arizona have that are the same age?

_____

b. A fossil is found in layer 7 in Utah. Another fossil is found in layer 6 in Arizona. Are they the same age?

              Yes   No

Use complete sentences to explain how you know.

_____

_____

_____

35—Slow Changes to the Earth's Surface

A [1]The surface of the earth changes as time goes by. [2]Sometimes, it can be transformed suddenly. [3]For example earthquakes and volcanic eruptions can result in sudden change. [4]However, many changes happen very slowly. [5]Forests can change into deserts over millions of years. [6]Deep *ravines*, like the Grand Canyon, can be cut out of solid rock by the force of running water. [7]In this lesson, you will learn about two ways the surface of the earth can change slowly: weathering and erosion.

B [8]**Weathering** is the natural process that breaks rocks into small pieces. [9]It takes work to break down rocks. [10]Think about smashing a rock into smaller pieces using a hammer. [11]That's hard work! [12]Over long periods of time, the wind can also apply large forces to rocks and wear them away. [13]Force is also applied to rocks by running water, waves, and rain.

C [14]Changes in temperature also cause weathering. [15]For example, rocks often crack when they cool down or heat up too fast. [16]Therefore, over very long periods of time, weathering can change rocks into fine particles.

D [17]As rocks are broken down by weathering into smaller and smaller pieces, they are more easily moved by the forces of nature. [18]This process is called erosion, and over time it makes huge changes to the surface of the earth. [19]**Erosion** is the movement of weathered rocks and soil by wind, water, and ice.

E [20]By itself, weathering can change the surface of the earth. [21]But weathering followed by erosion changes the surface much faster. [22]Look at the flow chart below. [23]It shows how the earth is changed by weathering and erosion. [24]In this case, it shows that we can start with rocks and end up with canyons or sand dunes!

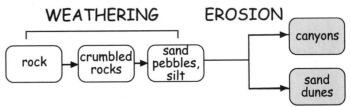

F [25]The bar graph below shows the speed of running water needed to move weathered rocks of different sizes.

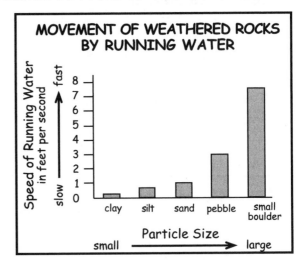

[26]Clay and silt particles are extremely small. [27]A silt particle is less than a thousandth of an inch in diameter! [28]Pebbles are small rocks. [29]Small boulders are about 1 foot across and weigh around 10 pounds. [30]Look at the bar graph. [31]How fast does the water need to go to move a small boulder?

1. For each statement, circle T or F for true or false. In the blanks, write the letters of the PARAGRAPH(s) that give the best evidence for your answer.

   a. Weathering happens before erosion.   T F ____ , ____

   b. You can weather a rock by using a hammer.   T F ____

   c. A ravine is the result of erosion caused by running water.   T F ____

   d. It takes faster moving water to move silt particles than to move sand particles.   T F ____

2. What is the most likely meaning of *ravines* as it is used in sentence 6?

   a. lakes

   b. holes

   c. narrow valleys

   d. mountains

3. What if the temperature goes from very cold to very hot to very cold many times over a long period of time? Use one or more complete sentences to explain what could happen to large rocks.

   _____

   _____

   _____

4. Consider a fast moving stream. Would you expect to find its bottom covered by clay and silt, or sand and pebbles?

   _____

5. The shoreline is made up of eroded rock particles of different sizes, as shown in the table below.

SHORELINE MATERIALS

Material	Size (mm)
Coarse sand	2
Medium sand	.6
Fine sand	.2
Silt	.1

Use the data in the table above to finish drawing the bar graph below comparing particle sizes.

SHORELINE MATERIALS BAR GRAPH

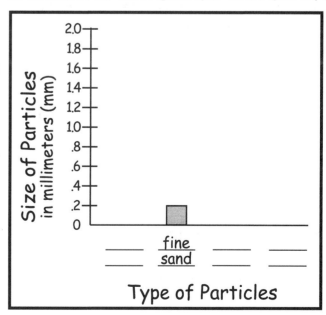

36—Fast Changes to the Earth's Surface

A [1]The earth's surface can change slowly over millions of years, or it can change suddenly. [2]In this lesson, you will learn about quick changes that can occur in minutes or hours.

B [3]Geologists have identified three major natural events that cause fast changes to the earth's surface. [4]They are volcanoes, landslides, and earthquakes.

C [5]The earth's crust is thin and solid. [6]Beneath the crust is molten rock called **magma**. [7]Sometimes, heat and pressure crack the crust, and magma breaks through to the surface. [8]When this happens, a **volcano** is formed. [9]The crack is called a **vent**.

D [10]When magma reaches the surface, it is called **lava**. [11]Lava flows out of the vent. [12]What do you think happens when lava reaches the air? [13]It cools down and turns into rock again. [14]What happens as more and more lava flows? [15]More and more rock forms. [16]The volcano gets bigger and higher. [17]Underwater volcanoes can get tall enough to reach the surface. [18]What is created when this happens? [19]An island. [20]Look at the flow chart below. [21]It shows how rock can form from magma.

Magma → Pressure → Vent → Lava flow → Rock

E [22]Fast changes in the earth's surface can also be produced by large movements of the earth's crust. [23]Huge sheets of rock called *plates* form the earth's crust. [24]Sometimes, there is a crack in a plate. [25]This crack is called a **fracture**. [26]If the rocks are moving slowly along the crack, the crack is called a **fault**. [27]When rocks suddenly slide along a fault, an **earthquake** is produced.

F [28]How do earthquakes make changes to the surface of the earth? [29]They create landslides and move large amounts of rock. [30]Earthquakes can also change the paths of rivers and cause huge sea waves called tidal waves.

G [31]A **seismograph** is an instrument used to measure movement in the earth's crust. [32]It *detects* both up-and-down and side-to-side motion. [33]It records information on a sheet of paper called a **seismogram**. [34]Compare the two seismograms below. [35]Seismogram *A* was recorded during an earthquake.

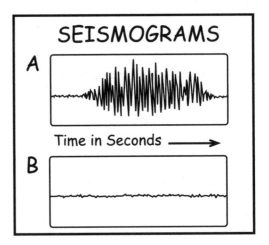

SEISMOGRAMS

A

Time in Seconds →

B

H [36]A **landslide** is the sudden movement of rocks shaken loose by heavy rains, melting snow, or earthquakes. [37]The earth's surface can be quickly changed by landslides. [38]They can fill in valleys and level mountains. [39]What force keeps rocks moving during a landslide?

1. For each statement, circle T or F for true or false. In each blank, write the letter of the PARAGRAPH that gives the best evidence for your answer.

   a. Volcanoes can build mountains.

   T F ___

   b. Heat does not come out of vents in the earth's surface.

   T F ___

   c. Faults form before fractures.

   T F ___

   d. The higher the lines on a seismogram, the stronger the earth's motion.   T F ___

2. What is the most likely meaning of *detects*, used in sentence 32?

   a. senses

   b. causes

   c. prevents

   d. removes

3. There are active and inactive volcanoes throughout the state of Hawaii. How might this information help you explain how our 50th state was formed? Use a complete sentence or two to answer.

   _____

   _____

   _____

   Write the letter of the paragraph that gives the best evidence for your answer. ___

4. During a landslide, in what direction does the land always slide? Use a complete sentence or two to answer.

   _____

   _____

   _____

5. Place the following terms in the flow chart to show which one might cause the next. *Earthquake, Fault, Tidal Wave, Fracture*

6. After the first shock waves from an earthquake are recorded on a seismogram, there are follow-up quakes called aftershocks. On the seismogram below, label the initial earthquake *E* and each of its aftershocks *A*.

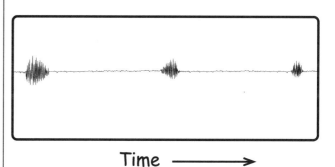

   Time ⟶

7. What can you say about the strength of aftershocks by looking at the data on the seismogram above? Use a complete sentence to explain your answer.

   _____

   _____

   _____

37—The Atmosphere and Weather

A [1]Our weather is created by differences in air temperature and pressure. [2]To understand this, we must first take a look at the **atmosphere**. [3]The atmosphere is the thin layer of gases covering the earth. [4]It is *transparent*. [5]We see through the atmosphere because it is made up of small gas particles that are not close together. [6]Nitrogen and oxygen gas make up most of earth's atmosphere.

[7]There are also small amounts of carbon dioxide and other gases. [8]What gas is there the most of?

GASES IN THE EARTH'S ATMOSPHERE

B [9]**Weather** describes what is happening in the atmosphere at a particular place on the surface of the earth. [10]Weather can be cold, hot, wet, dry, windy, or calm. [11]Before learning how the atmosphere produces weather, we need to know about air pressure.

C [12]Think of the water in a swimming pool. [13]The deeper you dive, the greater the water pressure on you. [14]The atmosphere also has weight. [15]Therefore, the more atmosphere above your head, the heavier it gets. [16]Look at the graph that follows. [17]Where is pressure least? [18]Where is it greatest? [19]Where would you expect to find the least air pressure, at the beach or on the top of a mountain? [20]Why would it be less at a mountaintop?

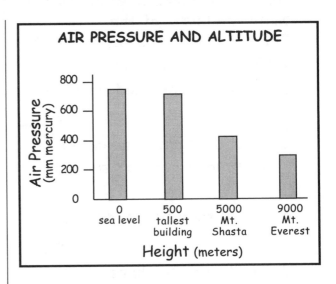

AIR PRESSURE AND ALTITUDE

D [21]Weather is made when large areas of atmosphere move. [22]The movement of air is caused by differences in air temperature and in air pressure.

E [23]High pressure air always moves towards areas of low pressure. [24]We call the *horizontal* movement of air "wind." [25]But the atmosphere also moves *vertically*. [26]When air gets warmer, it rises ↑. [27]The up and down movements of air are called air **currents**.

F [28]Does the sun heat the whole surface of the earth to the same temperature? No. [29]The area along the equator is very hot. [30]Does the air over the equator rise or sink? [31]Why do you think it rises?

G [32]The surface of the earth is heated unevenly. [33]Therefore, the atmosphere is always in motion. [34]The bigger the temperature or pressure difference between two areas, the more the air movement. [35]This air can reach high speeds and can carry rain or snow. [36]The more the air moves, the more noticeable is the weather!

1. For each statement, circle T or F for true or false. In each blank, write the number of the SENTENCE that gives the best evidence for your answer.

   a. Weather takes place within the oceans of the earth.   T F ____

   b. Air pressure is less on a boat than outside a flying airplane.
      T F ____

   c. The greater the temperature difference between two air masses, the stronger the wind.
      T F ____

2. What is the most likely meaning of *transparent* as it is used in sentence 4?

   a. clear
   b. solid
   c. dark
   d. light

3. Consider diagram *a* below. Draw an arrow that shows the direction the air would flow. Do the same for diagram *b*.

   a. 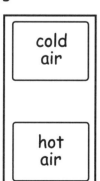   b.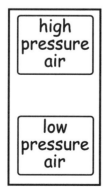

4. The arrows in the diagram below show how air currents move near the surface of the earth.

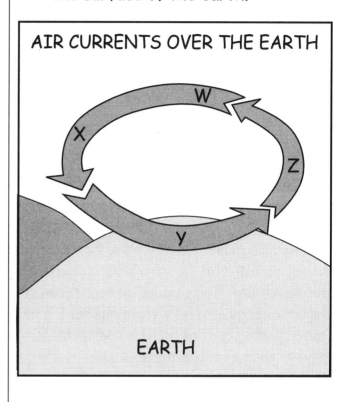

Use the diagram to help you answer the following.

   a. The air pressure is greatest at
      W   X   Y   Z

   b. The coldest air can be found at
      W   X   Y   Z

   c. Is the air at Y warmer or cooler than the air at X? _____

   d. The warmest air can be found at _____.

   e. Is the temperature of the air at Z getting warmer or cooler? _____

38—Measuring Temperature, Air Pressure, and Humidity

A [1]Temperature, air pressure, and humidity are important parts of the weather. [2]Each can be measured by a different tool, or **instrument**.

B [3]Gas particles in the atmosphere move around. [4]The warmer the gas, the faster the movement. [5]The temperature of the atmosphere is caused by the energy of its gas particles. [6]A **thermometer** is used to measure this energy. [7]When gas molecules move faster, they *collide* with, or hit, the tip of a thermometer more often. [8]Each *collision* transfers a little energy to the thermometer. [9]The more particles that hit the thermometer, the higher the temperature.

C [10]Air **pressure** is produced by the weight, or force, of the air pushing downward. [11]A **mercury barometer** is used to measure atmospheric pressure.

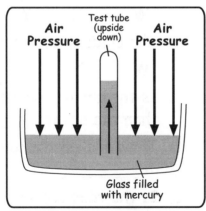

MERCURY BAROMETER

D [12]In the diagram above, what do the arrows pointing down *represent*? [13]They show air pressure caused by the weight of air pushing down. [14]Let's say the weight of air pushing down is increased. [15]Does the level of mercury in the glass go up or down? [16]What about the level of mercury in the test tube? [17]Does it go up or down? [18]As air pressure increases, it pushes down on the mercury in the glass and makes the mercury in the tube go up.

E [19]Air pressure is affected by **altitude**, or how high you are above the earth. [20]The higher the altitude, the more the air molecules are spread out. [21]The air is thinner, or less dense. [22]As you climb a mountain, will the mercury go up or down in a barometer tube? [23]Barometric pressure goes down. Why?

F [24]Air pressure is also affected by temperature. [25]Gases move faster in hot air than in cold air. [26]Fast moving gas spreads out and takes up more space. [27]Therefore, hot air is less dense than cold air. [28]Which produces more air pressure, warm or cold air? [29]As you traveled south from Alaska to the desert, the mercury in the tube would go down. [30]Can you explain why?

G [31]**Humidity** is a measure of water vapor. [32]Water vapor is the amount of water in the atmosphere. [33]As the atmosphere fills with water vapor, it becomes more humid. [34]Water vapor molecules take up more space than air molecules. [35]Why is humid air lighter than dry air? [36]Humid air is less dense.

H [37]Did you ever notice how humidity in the air affects your hair? [38]Hair stretches when it is damp. [39]The more humid the air, the longer the hair stretches. [40]In fact, humidity is measured by an instrument that uses hair! [41]In a **hygrometer**, a hair is attached to a needle. [42]As the hair stretches, the needle moves. [43]It points to the amount of humidity in the air.

1. For each statement, circle T or F for true or false. In each blank, write the letter of the PARAGRAPH that gives the best evidence for your answer.

   a. Temperature is a measure of the energy in the air. T F ____

   b. When air gets warmer, air pressure drops.   T F ____

   c. As altitude increases, air pressure becomes greater.
                                    T F ____

   d. Water vapor is heavier than air.
                                    T F ____

   e. Fast moving air weighs more than slow moving air.   T F ____

2. What is the most likely meaning of *represent*, as used in sentence 12?

   a produce

   b. point to

   c. stand for

   d. move to

3. Think about climbing a mountain. Why will there be less air pressure as you go higher? Use a complete sentence to explain your answer.

   _____

   _____

   _____

   Write the letter of the paragraph that gives the best evidence for your answer. ____

4. The data table shows how much water vapor is in the atmosphere at different temperatures. Use this data to complete the line graph below.

HUMIDITY

Temperature (°C)	Water vapor (g/kg of air)
10	10
20	15
30	30
40	50
50	80

LINE GRAPH OF
TEMPERATURE & WATER VAPOR

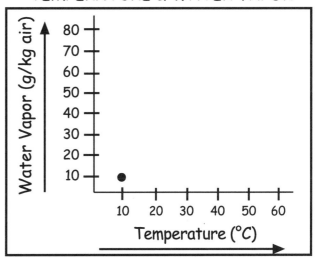

5. Use the table and line graph above to answer the following questions.

   a. When you connect the dots, the line is _____ .

      straight   curved

   b. At 60°C, the amount of water vapor held in the air will be _____ than the amount held at 50°C.

      greater   less

   c. Which holds less water?

      warmer air   colder air

39—Objects in the Sky

A [1]Earth science is more than the study of the earth by *geologists*. [2]It is also the study of the atmosphere by *meteorologists*, the oceans by *oceanographers*, and objects in the universe by *astronomers*.

B [3]In this lesson, you will learn about some of the objects in the sky. [4]What do you see up there? [5]You see clouds, birds, airplanes, the moon, stars, and the sun. [6]Some of these are quite close. [7]Birds seldom fly higher than very tall buildings. [8]Clouds are usually no more than two miles up. [9]Airplanes fly a little higher, sometimes up to eight miles. [10]But some objects are very far away. [11]The moon is about 240 thousand miles from the earth. [12]The sun is 93 million miles away!

C [13]Closer objects seem to move faster than distant objects. [14]The distance between you and a moving object affects how fast it seems to go. [15]Close objects, like flying insects, seem to zoom across the yard while far objects, like the moon, take the whole night to move across the sky. [16]It may surprise you to learn that an insect flies at about 5 miles per hour while the moon travels at 2300 m.p.h.!

D [17]When talking about the sky, astronomers refer to the universe. [18]Think of the **universe** as a huge space filled with all the objects in the sky. [19]The table at the upper right shows some objects found in the universe. [20]Which object is largest? [21]Which is smallest?

E [22]The universe has billions of stars. [23]Our sun is one of these stars. [24]Some

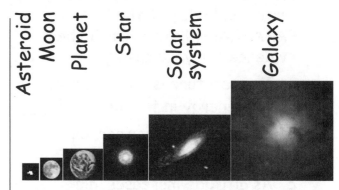

Asteroid Moon Planet Star Solar system Galaxy

stars have objects that *revolve* around them, such as **planets** and asteroids. [25]Earth is a planet that revolves around the sun. [26]An **asteroid** is a smaller object that also revolves around the sun.

F [27]Just as planets and asteroids revolve around a star, moons revolve around a planet. [28]The path taken by a planet, asteroid, or moon is called an **orbit**.

G [29]A **solar system** includes a star, all its asteroids, and planets with their moons. [30]A **galaxy** is a collection of billions of solar systems. [31]Earth is in the Milky Way Galaxy.

H [32]Seven of the nine planets in our solar system have moons. [33]Look at the table below. [34]Can you conclude anything about the diameter of a planet and the numbers of moons it has?

Name	Diameter in miles	# Moons
Mercury	3,000	0
Venus	7,500	0
Earth	8,000	1
Mars	4,000	2
Jupiter	88,500	26
Saturn	74,500	30
Uranus	31,500	18
Neptune	30,000	8
Pluto	2,500	1

PLANETS & MOONS

1. For each statement, circle T or F for true or false. In each blank, write the letter of the PARAGRAPH that gives the best evidence for your answer.

    a. Stars are studied by geologists.
        T F ____

    b. The closer a moving object, the faster it seems to go. T F ____

    c. Astronomers study the objects in the universe.   T F ____

    d. Stars are larger than their solar systems.   T F ____

2. What is the most likely meaning of *revolve* as used in paragraph E?

    a. move in a straight line

    c. move down

    b. move up

    d. move in a circle

3. Earth, Mars, Venus, and Saturn have something in common. They all share the same

    a. moons.

    c. orbit.

    b. star.

    d. asteroids.

4. Use the *Planets & Moons* table in the lesson to complete the following sentence.
    The larger planets tend to have
        more   fewer
    moons than smaller planets have.

    Is this true for all planets?
        Yes   No

5. In this table, the distance from each planet to the sun is given in astronomical units* (AU).

    *one AU = the distance from Earth to the sun, or 93 million miles.

Distance from the Sun

Planet	AU
Mercury	.4
Venus	.7
Earth	1
Mars	1.5
Jupiter	5
Saturn	9
Uranus	19
Neptune	30
Pluto	39

Use the table to answer the questions.

a. Which planet is closest to the Earth?

_____

b. Which is closer to Neptune?
        Uranus   Pluto

c. Which two planets are the same distance from Venus?

_____

_____

d. Which two planets have the greatest distance between them?

_____

_____

e. How far is Jupiter from the sun in astronomical units? _____

f. Fill in the multiplication problem to show how far Jupiter is from the sun.   **93** million miles

        X _____ AU

        = _____ million miles

40—The Sun

A [1]The sun provides the energy that is necessary to keep the earth warm. [2]Heat and light energy *radiate* from the sun and travel to the earth. [3]You have already learned that all living things depend on the energy of the sun to produce food. [4]Without the sun, plants could not grow and all life on earth would die. [5]In this lesson, you will learn more about the sun.

B [6]The sun is a star. [7]It is at the center of our solar system. [8]Nine planets travel around the sun along pathways called orbits. [9]The orbits are not exactly round. [10]An orbit is in the shape of an ellipse. [11]How would you describe an ellipse? [12]An **ellipse** is an egg-shaped circle.

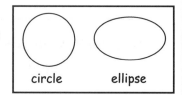

circle   ellipse

C [13]The orbit of each planet is a different size. [14]The farther a planet is from the sun, the larger its orbit. [15]It takes the earth 365 days to go around the sun. [16]Mars takes 687 days.

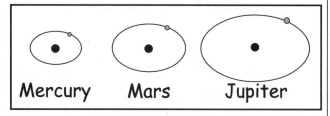

Mercury   Mars   Jupiter

D [17]Which planet would you expect to be the warmest—Mercury, Mars, or Jupiter? [18]Which do you think is the coldest? [19]Why do you think so?

E [20]The sun is extremely hot—its temperature is more than 5000 °C. [21]99% of the sun is made up of two elements, hydrogen and helium. [22]The sun is 5 billion years old. [23]Good news—it is expected to last another 5 billion years!

F [24]Look at the data table below. [25]It lists the five outer planets and gives their temperatures. [26]In general, what can you say about the temperature of a planet and its distance from the sun?

G [27]The data in the table was used to make the line graph below. [28]The outer planets are very cold. [29]In fact, the temperatures are far below zero. [30]In the graph, notice that the warmest temperature is –150° and the coldest is –240°.

SURFACE TEMPERATURE OF OUTER PLANETS

Planet	Temperature
Jupiter	-150°C
Saturn	-180°C
Uranus	-210°C
Neptune	-230°C
Pluto	-240°C

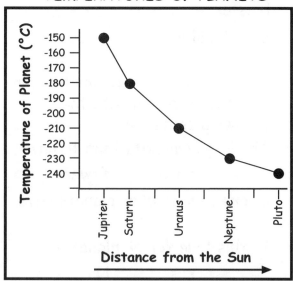

TEMPERATURES OF PLANETS

1. For each statement, circle T or F for true or false. In the blanks, write the number(s) of the SENTENCE(s) that gives the best evidence for your answer.

   a. The planet closest to the sun has the smallest orbit. T F ____

   b. An egg is shaped like an orbit.
      T F ____, ____

   c. The sun will live to be about 5 billion years old. T F ____, ____

   d. You would expect Jupiter to take longer than Mercury to complete an orbit. T F ____

2. What is the most likely meaning of *radiate* as it is used in sentence 2?

   a. move away

   b. return

   c. orbit

   d. visit

3. Imagine that the Earth has an orbit the size of Jupiter's. Complete the sentences below, comparing Earth to Jupiter.

   a. Earth's distance from the sun would _____

   _____ .

   b. Earth's temperature would

   _____

   _____ .

   c. Earth's plant and animal life would _____

   _____ .

4. If we discovered a planet farther than Pluto from the sun, what would you predict about its temperature? Use the *Temperatures of Planets* line graph in the lesson to help you.

   The new planet's temperature would be

   a. lower than Pluto's.

   b. higher than Pluto's.

   c. more than 240° C.

   d. less than –300° C.

5. Each planet takes a different amount of time to complete one orbit around the sun. Look at the table below. It shows the distance from the sun to each planet.

PLANETARY DATA

Name	Distance from the Sun in Millions of Miles	Orbit
Mercury	36	_____
Venus	67	_____
Earth	93	_____
Mars	141	_____
Jupiter	442	_____
Saturn	885	_____
Uranus	1780	_____
Neptune	2788	_____
Pluto	3667	_____

Complete the table above correctly by filling in the last column using the data listed below.

164 years	29 years	365 days
249 years	88 days	12 years
225 days	687 days	84 years

41—The Motion of Objects in the Universe

A [1]The universe is a *vast* space. [2]It is filled with huge galaxies made up of billions of stars. [3]Some of these stars have planets in orbit around them. [4]A **solar system** is made up of a star and the planets that revolve around it. [5]There are nine planets orbiting our star, the sun.

B [6]All the objects in the universe are in constant motion. [7]Galaxies move away from the center of the universe. [8]Solar systems move within their galaxy. [9]Planets move around their star, and moons travel around their planets. [10]Also, planets rotate like spinning tops! [11]What evidence is there that the earth is rotating? [12]The sun appears to move across the day sky, and the moon seems to move across the night sky.

C [13]As the earth rotates, it travels along its orbit around the sun.

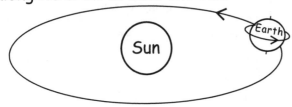

[14]It takes the earth 24 hours to make one rotation and 365 rotations to make one trip around the sun. [15]The length of time it takes a planet to complete one orbit around the sun is called a period. [16]The period of the earth is 365 days.

D [17]Powerful telescopes and other new technologies allow scientists to study objects in the universe. [18]Space probes have been sent to gather information from other planets. [19]Astronauts have already visited the moon, and NASA has sent probes to other planets.

E [20]Look at the tables below. [21]They show the size, number of moons, distance, and speed of nine planets. [22]Consider the distance of each planet from the sun. [23]Then think about long distances on earth. [24]For example, from Miami to Philadelphia is one thousand miles. [25]The United States is three thousand miles across. [26]It is 24

INNER PLANETS	Diameter of planet in miles	Moons	Speed in orbit (mph)	Millions of miles from the sun
Mercury	3,000	0	106,000	36
Venus	7,000	0	78,000	67
Earth	8,000	1	67,000	93
Mars	4,000	2	54,000	142

OUTER PLANETS	Diameter of planet in miles	Moons	Speed in orbit (mph)	Millions of miles from the sun
Jupiter	90,000	16	29,000	500
Saturn	75,000	18	22,000	900
Uranus	30,000	20	15,000	1,700
Neptune	30,000	8	21,000	2,800
Pluto	1,500	1	10,000	3,700

thousand miles around the earth, and 238 thousand miles to the moon. [27]You could go to the moon and back four times before you had traveled even one million miles! [28]The distance from Earth to sun is 93 times one million miles. [29]Does this give you a better idea of the enormous size of our solar system? [30]And if our solar system is so big, imagine how vast is the entire universe!

1. For each statement, circle T or F for true or false. In each blank, write the number of the SENTENCE that gives the best evidence for your answer.

   a. A star is at the center of a solar system.   T F ____

   b. Planets follow orbits around their moons.   T F ____

   c. Some objects in the sky do not move.   T F ____

   d. The earth takes 365 days to go around the sun.   T F ____

2. What is the most likely meaning of *vast* as used in sentences 26 and 30?

   a. tiny   c. very simple

   b. empty   d. very large

3. The stars seem to move slowly across the night sky. What does this tell you about the motion of the earth? Use a complete sentence to explain your answer.

   _____

   _____

   _____

   Write the letter of the paragraph that gives the best evidence for your answer. ____

4. Use the charts in the lesson to answer the following questions.

   a. Which outer planet is smaller than Earth?

   _____

b. Complete the following sentence:
As a planet gets farther from the sun, its speed in orbit

_____ .

c. Write the names of the 9 planets in order from smallest to largest.

_____

_____

_____

_____

_____

_____

_____

_____

_____

5. Complete the bar graph to show each planet's distance from the sun.

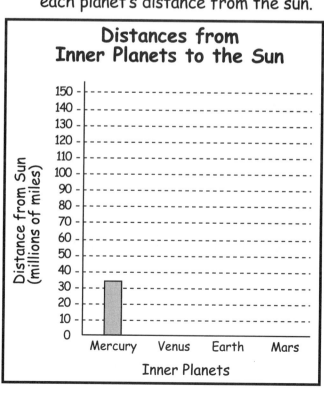

ANSWERS

Unit I: Physical Science

Lesson 1, pp. 2–3

1. a. T <u>B</u>, b. F <u>B</u>, c. F <u>E</u>

2. a. Yes, b. No, c. No

3. a

4. b

5. c

6. (Information is given in the chart under paragraph D.)

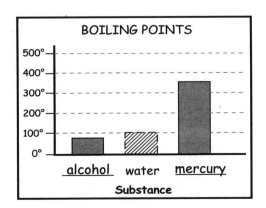

BOILING POINTS

alcohol   water   mercury

Substance

Lesson 2, pp. 4–5

1. a. T <u>B</u>, b. F <u>A</u>, c. F <u>D</u>, <u>E</u>

2. b (see *Using a Thermometer* diagram)

3. a, <u>14</u>

4. <u>F</u>, <u>C</u>
summer (most likely, since 32° C is about 90° F; possibly spring or fall, depending on your geographical location)

5. 1.8 (or 2), 2.1 (or 2); 2.3 (or 2 1/2)

6. b

7. see F on thermometer

8. see R on thermometer

9. F, <u>22</u>

Lesson 3, pp. 6–7

1. a. F <u>6</u> b. T <u>7</u>, c. T <u>15</u>, d. T <u>13</u>

2. c

3. b

4. (Accept any reasonable answers. Indoor examples: basketball, table tennis, badminton, volleyball, etc. Outdoor examples: skiing, tennis, baseball, football, etc. Some sports could be either indoors or outdoors, e.g., ice hockey.)

5. Metals: gold, copper, silver, etc. Nonmetals: plastic, wood, glass, cloth, etc.

Lesson 4, pp. 8–9

1. a. T <u>7</u>, b. F <u>8</u>, c. F <u>11</u>

2. As ice melts, the atoms move more quickly (slide past each other, etc.). <u>9</u>, <u>10</u>

3. d

4.

Utility Vehicles			
	Miles per gallon (fuel)	Number of Passengers	Price of Vehicles
Best	MV	MV	PT
Worst	SUV	PT	SUV

°C

110
105
100
95
90
85
80
75
70
65
60
55
50
45
40
35
30
25
20
15
10
5
0
-5
-10
-15
-20

R

F

5. (Spacing of atoms: accept illustrations showing that atoms spread out more as state changes from solid to liquid to gas; Movement of Atoms: accept any wording that describes motion from slowest to quickest.)

States of Matter		
State	Spacing of atoms	Movement of atoms
solid	⬡⬡⬡⬡	very slow
liquid	ᵒ ᵒ ᵒ ᵒ	slow
gas	ᵒ ᵒ ᵒ	quick

Lesson 5, pp. 10–11

1. a. T <u>A</u>; b. F <u>C</u>, <u>D</u>; c. F <u>D</u>; d. T <u>F</u>

2. $65

3. d, <u>14</u>

4. Yes, <u>F</u>

5. Freezing is the change in state from a liquid to a solid.

6. c

7. a. <u>S</u>, b. <u>L</u>, c. <u>G</u>, d. <u>S</u>

8. Heat the mirror. (Use a blow dryer, etc.; also, using a ventilation fan could prevent vapor build-up.) <u>G</u>

Lesson 6, pp. 12–13

1. a. T <u>17</u>, <u>18</u>; b. F <u>6</u>; c. F <u>9</u>

2. a. G5 (given), b. B2, c. D4, d. G2

3. c

4. <u>B</u> <u>4</u>

5.

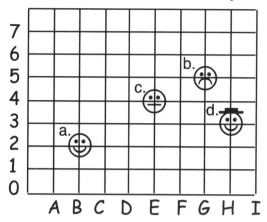

Finding the Position of an Object

6. a. <u>O</u> <u>2</u>, b. <u>A</u> <u>7</u>, c. <u>A</u> <u>9</u>, d. <u>L</u> <u>9</u>

Lesson 7, pp. 14–15

1. a. T <u>4</u>; b. F <u>18</u>, <u>22</u>; c. T <u>29</u>

2. a. Y; b. N; c. N

3. c, <u>22</u>

4. (Accept answers that show a large weight for B and small arrows for A and C—arrow C should be slightly larger than arrow A.)

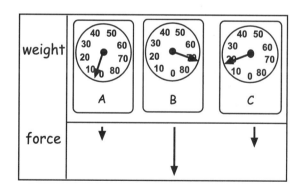

5. Note: Accept any answers that make sense within the context of the chart.

	small force	large force
using a hammer	→ tapping	→ pounding
ocean	→ ripple	→ tidal wave
sounds	→ whisper	→ scream

6. A driver slows the car with the force of pushing or stepping on the car's brakes (which causes friction). <u>B</u>

Lesson 8, pp. 16–17

1. a. T <u>16</u>, b. F <u>18</u>, c. T <u>14</u>

2. a. Y, b. Y, c. Y, d. N

3. b

4. b

5.

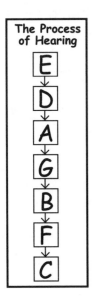

Lesson 9, pp. 18–19

1. a. F <u>C</u>, b. T <u>A</u>, c. T <u>E</u>, d. F <u>C</u>

2. a. A, b. B, c. A

3. Air particles compressed by a whistle would be closer together. Air particles compressed by a tuba would be farther apart.

4.

	Tone	Volume
Lion	Low	High
Mouse	High	Low

The roar of a lion has a low tone and high volume. The squeak of a mouse has a high tone and low volume.

5. c

6. c

7. The string vibrates faster.

Lesson 10, pp. 20–21

1. a. T <u>B</u>; b. F <u>C</u>; c. F <u>G</u>, <u>I</u>; d. F <u>J</u>

2. a

3. Yes. Seeing and hearing are senses, and they require energy. Smelling is a sense too, so it probably also takes energy. (Also, sentence 1 says energy is needed to make anything happen.) <u>A</u>, <u>B</u>

4. a, d (b is incorrect because paragraphs F, G, and I say that light rays can be bounced or bent; there is no evidence for c)

5. a. <u>3</u>, b. <u>1</u>

6. A pencil looks broken because the light goes from air through water and back through air.

7. b

Lesson 11, pp. 22-23

1. a. F <u>9</u>, b. F <u>7</u>, c. F <u>1</u>, <u>27</u>

2. d

3. Their temperatures are the same. (If atoms of the same substance are vibrating at the same speed, they must be at the same temperature.) <u>G</u>

4.

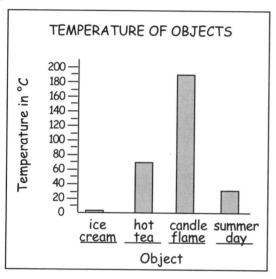

5.

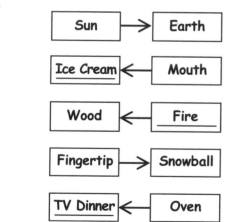

Lesson 12, pp. 24-25

1. a. T <u>A</u>, b. F <u>C</u>, c. F <u>E</u>, d. F <u>E</u>

2. d

3. d, <u>15</u>

4. Yes, because friction is produced in a poor conductor. Friction produces heat. <u>E</u>

5. (Accept arrangements in which the three lights are connected between battery and switch.)

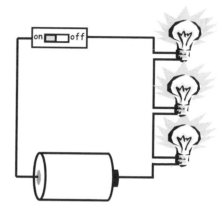

Lesson 13, pp. 26-27

1. a. F <u>9</u>, b. T <u>3</u>, c. T <u>4</u>, d. F <u>11</u>

2. a

3.

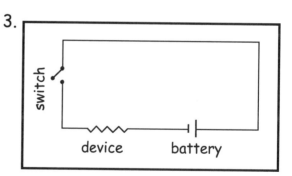

4.

5. a. No
   b. Off
   c. closed
   d.

6.
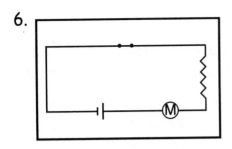

Lesson 14, pp. 28–29

1. a. T <u>10</u>, <u>12</u>; b. F <u>9</u>, <u>10</u>; c. T <u>11</u>;
   d. F <u>11</u>; e. F <u>30</u>

2. b

3. a. decreases
   b. increases
   c. decreases

4.
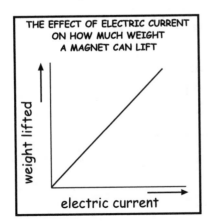

5. (See chart below; also accept labels switched: weight on horizontal axis and current on vertical axis.)

THE EFFECT OF ELECTRIC CURRENT
ON HOW MUCH WEIGHT
A MAGNET CAN LIFT

weight lifted

electric current

Unit II: Life Science

Lesson 15, p. 32–33

1. a. T <u>2</u>, b. T <u>5</u>, c. F <u>11</u>, d. F <u>1</u>
   (Living trees are organisms, but logs are parts that are no longer living.)

2. c

3. (Accept any reasonable answers. Examples appear below.)

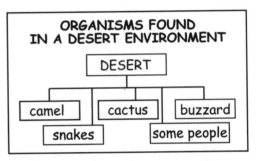

4.

SURVIVAL NEEDS OF ORGANISMS			
	Food	Shelter	Climate
Eagle	Mice	Tree	Cool
Seal	Fish	Ocean	Cold
Spider	Insects	Web	Warm

5. Rabbits need a warm place to live, air to breathe, water to drink, and food to eat.
   <u>C</u>

6. It is very cold at the South Pole, and there is not much food, shelter, or water for drinking.

7. In the rain forest, there is a lot of food, shelter, and water.

Lesson 16, p. 34–35

1. a. T <u>15</u>, b. F <u>9</u>, c. T <u>17</u>, d. T <u>17</u>,
   e. F <u>15</u>, f. T <u>9</u>

2. a. <u>9</u>

3. (Accept any reasonable answer.) Example: <u>Grassland</u>: <u>gophers, sheep, rabbits, grasses, deer</u>

4. <u>Tundra</u>

5.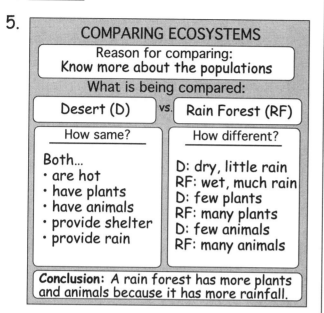

5. (Snakes and Monkeys labels may be reversed.)

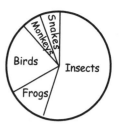

Lesson 18, pp. 38–39

1. a. F <u>17</u>; b. T <u>15</u>, <u>16</u>; c. T <u>23</u>; d. T <u>8</u>

2. a

3. nucleus, cell membrane, cytoplasm, and mitochondria

4. T
   <u>B</u>

5. c

6. (Accept any correctly labelled drawings resembling the nucleus, cell membrane, cell wall, mitochondria, vacuole, chloroplasts, and cytoplasm.)

7. Humans do not need cell walls because they have skeletons for support.

8. Plants get their coloring from their chloroplasts, which are green. <u>29</u>

Lesson 17, pp. 36–37

1. a. T <u>A</u>, b. T <u>B</u>, c. F <u>C</u>, d. F <u>D</u>, e. T <u>C</u>

2. b

3. a. <u>I</u> You blink without thinking about it. Babies blink when they are born.
   b. <u>L</u> A baby learns that when it cries it gets what it wants.
   c. <u>L</u> A dog learns that when it stands near food and whines it will get a snack.
   d. <u>I</u> You don't have to think about pulling away from something that's too hot.

4. (Sparrow and Finch labels may be reversed.)

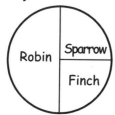

Lesson 19, pp. 40–41

1. a. T <u>2</u>; b. F <u>2</u>, <u>3</u>; c. F <u>4</u>; d. F <u>8</u>, <u>9</u>

2. b

3. The plant would die. <u>5</u>

4. d

5. Elevating a plant would help it get more sunlight and CO_2.
   <u>B</u>

6.

PARTS OF A PLANT

Part	If the part were missing The plant would...	What is its function? The part helps...
Leaf	not trap energy or take in CO_2.	trap energy.
Trunk	not get off the ground.	hold the tree up (elevate it).
Stem	not hold up its leaves or flowers.	hold the flower up (elevate it).
Root	fall over; not get water & minerals.	anchor the plant; get water.

Lesson 20, pp. 42–43

1. a. T 20, b. F 13, c. F 4, d. T 18

2. c

3. No. 11

4. [sun → plant → starch → animal]

5. (Any item may appear in the top, as long as items retain these relationships.)

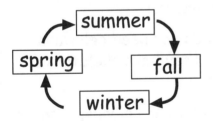

6. (Accept other rotational arrangements as long as they keep these relationships.)

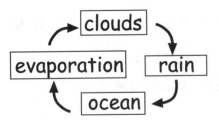

Lesson 21, pp. 44–45

1. a. T 3, b. T 18, c. F 39, d. F 32

2. c

3. c

4. An animal can smell smoke and feel heat, and will run away from a fire.

5. a. Yes; b. No; c. Yes; d. No

6. (Accept other responses if well supported; e.g., a test could cause a "stomachache," an internal response.)

SCHOOL BEHAVIOR

Stimulus	Internal	External	Response
Hunger	X		
Fire alarm		X	
Home-work		X	
Thirst	X		
Test		X	

Lesson 22, pp. 46–47

1. a. T 13, 16; b. F 2; c. T 28; d. F 29

2. c

3. Seeing and hearing can warn you that cars are coming.

4. a

5.

Sense Organ	Problem with Organ	Effect on the Animal
Ear	infection	harder to _hear_
Lungs	asthma	harder to _breathe_
Brain	stroke	harder to _act, think_
Muscles	sprain	harder to _walk, move_
Bone	broken	harder to _stand, walk, move_

6. a. sight, smell, touch
   b. sight, smell
   c. sight, sound
   d. sight, sound
   e. sight, smell, sound
   f. sight, smell, taste

7. stimulus:
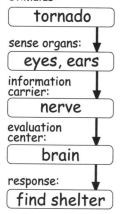

Lesson 23, pp. 48–49

1. a. F <u>1</u>, b. T <u>14</u>, c. T <u>9</u>, d. T <u>19, 20</u>

2. b

3. c
   <u>C, D</u> (see sentences 17 and 29)

4. Bright colors and smells of flowers attract insects.

5. The function of a flower is to produce pollen and attract birds and insects.

6.
COMPARING PLANTS		
What is being compared:		
Flowering Plant	vs.	Conifer
How same?		How different?
Both… • produce seeds • pollinate • grow seeds • produce seedlings • need water • need sun		C: have needles F: have leaves C: have cones F: have flowers C: stay green F: lose leaves C: wind pollinates F: animals pollinate
Conclusion: Conifers and flowering plants reproduce the same way but use different structures.		

Lesson 24, pp. 50–51

1. a. T <u>F</u>, <u>G</u>; b. F <u>E</u>; c. T <u>C</u>; d. F <u>F</u>, <u>G</u>

2. c

3. Cycles have no beginning or end. Death is an end. <u>E</u>

4. a. No   b. No

5.
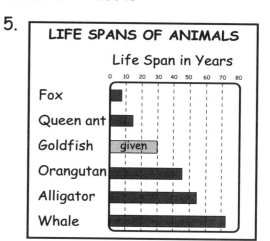

Lesson 25, pp. 52–53

1. a. T <u>A</u>, b. F <u>E</u>, c. F <u>E</u>, <u>F</u>

2. a

3. <u>inherited</u>
   Inherited traits come directly from parents, and learned traits come from the environment. <u>E</u>

4.
Animal Traits

Animal Trait	Inherited	Learned
Size of a cat's paw	✔	
A dog's tricks		✔
Color of insect wing	✔	
Shape of shark's tooth	✔	
Hunting		✔

5.   **Human Traits**

Human Trait	Inherited	Learned
Eye color	✔	
Hair color	✔	
Reading ability		✔
Playing hockey		✔
Height	✔	
Dancing		✔
Cooking		✔
Curly hair	✔	

6.

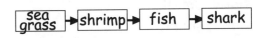

7.

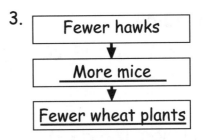

Lesson 26, pp. 54–55

1. a. F <u>6</u>; b. T <u>7</u>; c. T <u>3</u>, <u>5</u>; d. F <u>8</u>

2. b

3. Plants get their energy from sunlight. Without the sun, plants would die. <u>3</u>

4. No. Animals get energy from eating plants. They also get energy from eating animals that eat plants. Without plants, animals cannot get energy.

5.

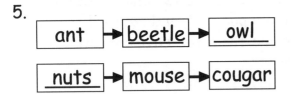

Lesson 27, pp. 56–57

1. a. F <u>C</u>, b. F <u>E</u>, c. T <u>E</u>, d. T <u>H</u>

2. c

3.

Fewer hawks

↓

More mice

↓

Fewer wheat plants

4. If there were more plants, there would be less water and less room for fish to live in.

5. There would not be any water left because the pond would fill up with mud.

Lesson 28, pp. 58–59

1. a. F <u>A</u>, b. T <u>E</u>, c. T <u>E</u>

2. d

3. The settlers made their own environment more comfortable. However, they destroyed homes and food for other animals.

4. It keeps people from harming the environment.

5.

Animals	Number
Zebras	50
Giraffes	20
Hippo-potamuses	15
Lions	10
Tigers	5

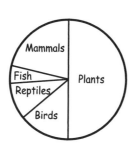

Unit III: Earth Science

Lesson 29, pp. 62–63

1. a. F <u>3</u>, b. F <u>24</u>, c. F <u>22</u>

2. c

3. mile, <u>20</u>

4.

What is studied	Science	Scientist
rocks	<u>geology</u>	<u>geologist</u>
planets, <u>stars</u>	<u>astronomy</u>	astronomer
<u>weather</u>	meteorology	<u>meteorologist</u>
oceans	<u>oceanography</u>	<u>oceanographer</u>

5. a. outer core
   b. mantle
   c. crust
   d. inner core
   e. surface

6. a. height, temperature
   b. 2
   c. The temperature gets lower.
   d. –20°
   e. (Accept from <u>12</u>° to <u>14</u>°)

Lesson 30, pp. 64–65

1. a. F <u>16</u>, b. F <u>10</u>, c. T <u>31</u>

2. a

3. c

4. a

5. a. oxygen
      It is the largest piece.
   b. iron
      The pieces look close to the same size.
   c. Some of the pieces would be too small to see.

6.

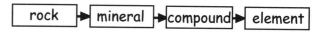

rock → mineral → compound → element

Lesson 31, pp. 66–67

1. a. F <u>4</u>; b. T <u>19, 20</u>; c. F <u>25</u>

2. b

3. a. talc
   b. quartz
   c. talc
   d. hematite (iron)
   e. hardness, color

4. <u>Hornblend</u>

5. Find all minerals that are white and have a hardness of 4. Then check the streak and luster.

6. (Accept any reasonable answer of four-word scale and ratings for activities.)

Lesson 32, pp. 68–69

1. a. T <u>6</u>, <u>7</u>;   b. F <u>12</u>, <u>13</u>;   c. F <u>13</u>, <u>14</u>

2. a, <u>6</u>

3. sedimentary
   The pressure from the piled up sediment cements the small pieces together.

4.

THE ROCK CYCLE

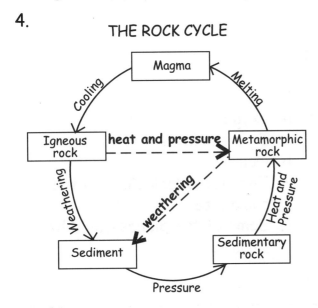

5. Marble can be weathered back into sediment. Pressure and heat can turn the sediment back into limestone.

Lesson 33, pp. 70–71

1. a. T <u>2</u>, <u>3</u>;   b. T <u>11</u>;   c. T <u>15</u>

2. d

3. False
   About half is made up of gas (air) and liquid (water).

4. No
   Humus is made of once-living material, and no life has been found on the moon.

5. Asian, Indian, South American, North American, Arabian, Australian, African

6.

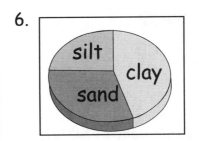

Lesson 34, pp. 72–73

1. a. F <u>A</u>,   b. T <u>E</u>,   c. F <u>F</u>,   d. T <u>D</u>

2. b

3. Organisms are preserved where it is very hot and dry or very cold. Rain forests are very wet.
   <u>H</u>

4. a. 5. (Arizona layers 1, 2, 3, 5, and 6 have patterns that also appear in the layers in Utah.)
   b. Yes
   Both have the same pattern, so they must be the same age.

Lesson 35, pp. 74–75

1. a. T <u>D</u>, <u>E</u>;   b. F <u>B</u>;   c. T <u>A</u>;   d. F <u>F</u>

2. b

3. The rocks crack into smaller and smaller particles by weathering.

4. sand and pebbles

5.

SHORELINE MATERIALS BAR GRAPH

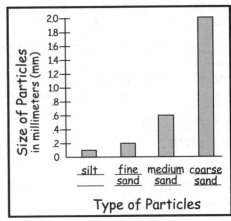

Lesson 36, pp. 76–77

1. a. T <u>D</u>, b. F <u>D</u>, c. F <u>E</u>, d. T <u>G</u>

2. a

3. It was formed by the buildup of cooled lava underwater until enough reached the surface to form islands.
   <u>D</u>

4. Gravity pulls loose objects down towards the earth.

5.

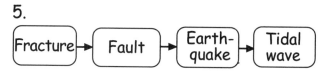

6.

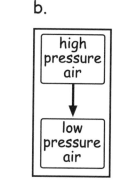

Time ⟶

7. The aftershocks are not as strong as the first earthquake.

Lesson 37, pp. 78–79

1. a. F <u>9</u>, b. F <u>15</u>, c. T <u>34</u>

2. a

3. a.   b.

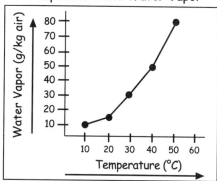

4. a. Y, b. W, c. warmer, d. Y,
   e. cooler

Lesson 38, pp. 80–81

1. a. T <u>B</u>, b. T <u>F</u>, c. F <u>E</u>, d. F <u>G</u>,
   e. F <u>F</u>

2. c

3. There is less air above you.
   <u>E</u>

4.

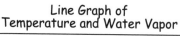

Line Graph of
Temperature and Water Vapor

5. a. curved; b. greater; c. colder air

Lesson 39, pp. 82–83

1. a. F <u>A</u>, b. T <u>C</u>, c. T <u>A</u>, d. F <u>G</u>

2. d

3. b

4. The larger planets tend to have <u>more</u> moons than the smaller planets do.
   No (Some small planets have more moons than larger planets do.)

5. a. Venus
   b. Pluto
   c. Mercury and Earth
   d. Mercury and Pluto
   e. <u>5</u> AU
   f. 93 x <u>5</u> = <u>465</u> million miles

Lesson 40, pp. 84–85

1. a. T <u>14</u>;   b. T <u>10</u>, <u>12</u>;   c. F <u>22</u>, <u>23</u>;
   d. T <u>14</u>

2. a

3. (Accept any reasonable answers
   similar to those below.)
   a. be greater.
   b. be lower.
   c. stop.

4. a

5.

PLANETARY DATA

Name	Distance from the Sun in Millions of Miles	Orbit
Mercury	36	<u>88 days</u>
Venus	67	<u>225 days</u>
Earth	93	<u>365 days</u>
Mars	141	<u>687 days</u>
Jupiter	442	<u>12 years</u>
Saturn	885	<u>29 years</u>
Uranus	1780	<u>84 years</u>
Neptune	2788	<u>164 years</u>
Pluto	3667	<u>249 years</u>

Lesson 41, pp. 86–87

1. a. T <u>4</u>,   b. F <u>9</u>,   c. F <u>6</u>,   d. T <u>14</u>

2. d

3. The earth is rotating.
   <u>B</u>

4. a. <u>Pluto</u>; b. <u>decreases</u>; c. Pluto,
   Mercury, Mars, Venus, Earth,
   Uranus/Neptune (about equal),
   Saturn, Jupiter

5.
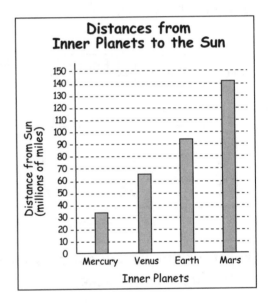